The Growth and Influence of Islam
IN THE NATIONS OF ASIA AND CENTRAL ASIA

Azerbaijan

The Growth and Influence of Islam
IN THE NATIONS OF ASIA AND CENTRAL ASIA

Afghanistan

Azerbaijan

Bangladesh

Indonesia

Islam in Asia: Facts and Figures

Islamism and Terrorist Groups in Asia

Kazakhstan

The Kurds

Kyrgyzstan

Malaysia

Muslims in China

Muslims in India

Muslims in Russia

Pakistan

Tajikistan

Turkmenistan

Uzbekistan

The Growth and Influence of Islam
In the Nations of Asia and Central Asia

Azerbaijan

Gerald Robbins

Mason Crest Publishers
Philadelphia

Produced by OTTN Publishing, Stockton, New Jersey

Mason Crest Publishers
370 Reed Road
Broomall, PA 19008
www.masoncrest.com

First printing

1 3 5 7 9 8 6 4 2

Library of Congress Cataloging-in-Publication Data

Robbins, Gerald.
  Azerbaijan / Gerald Robbins.
     p. cm. — (Growth and influence of Islam in the nations of Asia and Central Asia)
  Includes bibliographical references and index.
  ISBN 1-59084-878-0
  1. Azerbaijan—Juvenile literature. I. Title. II. Series.
  DK692.3.R63 2005
  947.54—dc22

                              2004019825

Table of Contents

Dr. Harvey Sicherman, president and director of the Foreign Policy Research Institute, is the author of such books as *America the Vulnerable: Our Military Problems and How to Fix Them* (2002) and *Palestinian Autonomy, Self-Government and Peace* (1993).

Introduction

by Dr. Harvey Sicherman

America's triumph in the Cold War promised a new burst of peace and prosperity. Indeed, the decade between the demise of the Soviet Union and the destruction of September 11, 2001, proved deceptively hopeful. Today, of course, we are more fully aware—to our sorrow—of the dangers and troubles no longer just below the surface.

The Muslim identities of most of the terrorists at war with the United States have also provoked great interest in Islam as well as the role of religion in politics. It is crucial for Americans not to assume that Osama bin Laden's ideas are identical to those of most Muslims or, for that matter, that most Muslims are Arabs. A truly world religion, Islam claims hundreds of millions of adherents, from every ethnic group scattered across the globe. This book series covers the growth and influence of Muslims in Asia and Central Asia.

A glance at the map establishes the extraordinary coverage of our authors. Every climate and terrain may be found, along with every form of human society, from the nomadic groups of the Central Asian steppes to highly sophisticated cities such as Singapore, New Delhi, and Shanghai. The economies of the nations examined in this series are likewise highly diverse. In some, barter systems are still used; others incorporate modern stock markets. In some of the countries, large oil reserves hold out the prospect of prosperity. Other countries, such as India and China, have progressed by moving from a government-controlled to a more market-based economic system. Still other countries have built wealth on service and shipping.

Central Asia and Asia is a heavily armed and turbulent area. Three of its states (China, India, and Pakistan) are nuclear powers, and one (Kazakhstan) only recently rid itself of nuclear weapons. But it is also a place where the horse and mule remain indispensable instruments of war. All of the region's states have an extensive history of conflict, domestic and international, old and new. Afghanistan, for example, has known little but invasion and civil war over the past two decades.

Governments include dictatorships, democracies, and hybrids without a name; centralized and decentralized administrations; and older patterns of tribal and clan associations. The region is a veritable encyclopedia of political expression.

Although such variety defies easy generalities, it is still possible to make several observations. First, the geopolitics of Central Asia and Asia reflect the impact of empires and the struggles of post-imperial independence. Central Asia, a historic corridor for traders and soldiers, was the scene of Russian expansion well into Soviet times. While Kazakhstan's leaders participated in the historic meeting of December 25, 1991, that dissolved the Soviet Union, the rest of the region's newly independent republics hardly expected it. They have found it difficult to grapple with a sometimes tenuous independence, buffeted by a strong residual Russian influence, the absence of settled institutions, the temptation of newly valuable natural resources, and mixed populations lacking a solid national identity. The shards of the Soviet Union have often been sharp—witness the Russian war in Chechnya—and sometimes fatal for those ambitious to grasp them.

An Azerbaijani man wears a tall *papakha*, a traditional hat made from astrakhan wool.

Moving further east, one encounters an older devolution, that of the half-century since the British Raj dissolved into India and Pakistan (the latter giving violent birth to Bangladesh in 1971). Only recently, partly under the impact of the war on terrorism, have these nuclear-armed neighbors and adversaries found it possible to renew attempts at reconciliation. Still further east, Malaysia shares a British experience, but Indonesia has been influenced by its Dutch heritage. Even China defines its own borders along the lines of the Qing empire (the last pre-republican dynasty) at its most expansionist (including Tibet and Taiwan). These imperial histories lie heavily upon the politics of the region.

A second aspect worth noting is the variety of economic experimentation afoot in the area. State-dominated economic strategies, still in the ascendant, are separating government from the actual running of commerce and industry. "Privatization," however, is frequently a byword for crony capitalism and corruption. Yet in dynamic economies such as that of China, as well as an increasingly productive India, hundreds of millions of people have dramatically improved both their standard of living and their hope for the future. All of them aspire to benefit from international trade. Competitive advantages, such as low-cost labor (in some cases trained in high technology) and valuable natural resources (oil, gas, and minerals), promise much. This is indeed a revolution of rising expectations, some of which are being satisfied.

Yet more than corruption threatens this progress. Population increase, even though moderating, still overwhelms educational and employment opportunities. Many countries are marked by extremes of wealth and poverty, especially between rural and urban areas. Dangerous jealousies threaten ethnic groups (such as anti-Chinese violence in Indonesia). Hopelessly overburdened public services portend turmoil. Public health, never adequate, is harmed further by environmental damage to critical resources (such as the Aral Sea). By and large, Central Asian and Asian countries are living well beyond their infrastructures.

Third and finally, Islam has deeply affected the states and peoples of the region. Indonesia is the largest Muslim state in the world, and India hosts the second-largest Muslim population. Islam is not only the official religion of many states, it is the very reason for Pakistan's existence. But Islamic practices and groups vary: the well-known Sunni and Shiite groups are joined by energetic Salafi (Wahabi) and Sufi movements. Over the last 20 years especially, South and Central Asia have become battlegrounds for competing Shiite (Iranian) and Wahabi (Saudi) doctrines, well financed from abroad and aggressively antagonistic toward non-Muslims and each other. Resistance to the Soviet invasion of Afghanistan brought these groups battle-tested warriors and organizers. The war on terrorism has exposed just how far-reaching and active the new advocates of holy war (jihad) can be. Indonesia, in particular, is the scene of rivalry between an older, tolerant Islam and the jihadists. But Pakistan also faces an Islamic identity crisis. And India, wracked by sectarian strife, must hold together its democratic framework despite Muslim and Hindu extremists. This newly significant struggle within Islam, superimposed on an older Muslim history, will shape political and economic destinies throughout the region and beyond. Hence, the focus of our series.

We hope that these books will enlighten both teacher and student about a critical subject in a critical area of the world. Central Asia and Asia would be important in their own right to Americans; arguably, after 9/11, they became vital to our national security. And the enduring impact of Islam is a crucial factor we must understand. We at the Foreign Policy Research Institute hope these books will illuminate both the facts and the prospects.

A group of tourists visit the Ateshgyakh Fire Temple, located about 15 miles (25 km) outside of modern Azerbaijan's capital, Baku. Flaming torches of natural gas seep through the ground of the Apsheron Peninsula in several places; they were once believed to have miraculous or divine power in a region where the fire-religion Zoroastrianism was prevalent in ancient times. The name *Azerbaijan* is believed by some researchers to mean "land of fires."

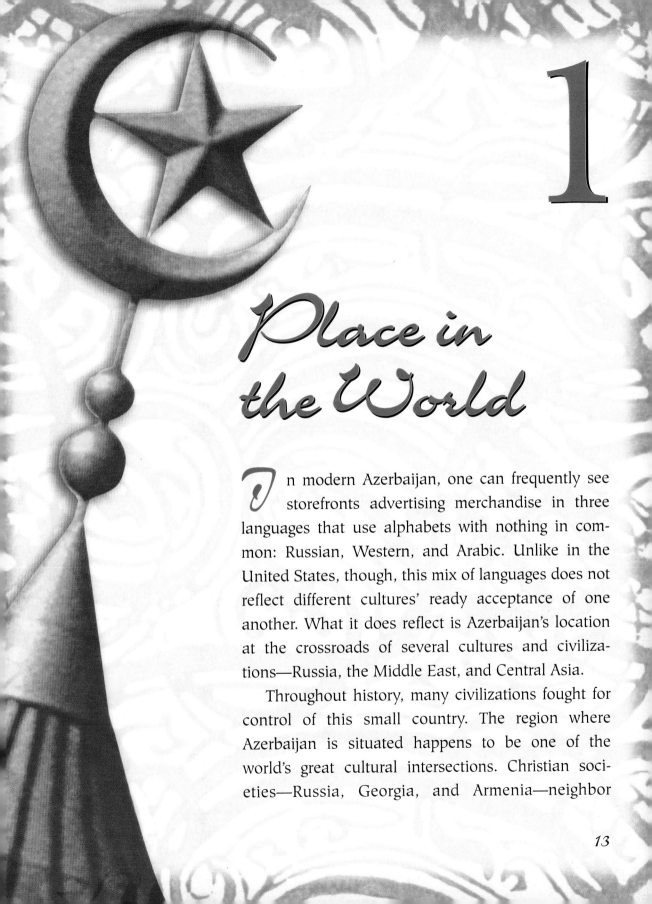

1

Place in the World

In modern Azerbaijan, one can frequently see storefronts advertising merchandise in three languages that use alphabets with nothing in common: Russian, Western, and Arabic. Unlike in the United States, though, this mix of languages does not reflect different cultures' ready acceptance of one another. What it does reflect is Azerbaijan's location at the crossroads of several cultures and civilizations—Russia, the Middle East, and Central Asia.

Throughout history, many civilizations fought for control of this small country. The region where Azerbaijan is situated happens to be one of the world's great cultural intersections. Christian societies—Russia, Georgia, and Armenia—neighbor

Azerbaijan to its north and west, while Muslim Turkey and Iran border the south. Since ancient times, ethnic conflicts have frequently occurred throughout this area, and so Greeks, Persians, Turks, Mongols, and Russians have all viewed the country as a key **borderland** that shielded their domains from enemy invasion.

Religious and Cultural Challenges

Azerbaijan's culture is predominantly Islamic, but its history and social character have been largely formed by non-Muslim influences. Christianity had already established a presence when Islam was introduced to Azerbaijan in the seventh century A.D. In fact, Christianity was the state religion of a kingdom that existed within present-day Azerbaijani territory. The other major faith in the region before the arrival of Islam was Zoroastrianism, whose religious symbol, a burning flame, also happens to be the national symbol of Azerbaijan. Fire is a fitting emblem for Azerbaijan: it represents not only the abundance of oil within its domain, but also represents an enduring national character that has been able to survive centuries of religious and cultural intrusions.

Islam has had less of an influence on modern Azerbaijan than it has had on other nearby Muslim countries. This is largely due to Russia's 200-year-long colonial legacy. The Russians conquered Azerbaijan in the early 19th century, making it a part of the Czarist empire, and later the Soviet Union. During this time ties between Azerbaijan and other Islamic countries withered, leaving a big gap in religious knowledge and practice. The Russians saw Islam as a backward culture and looked down upon its traditions. Western customs gradually replaced the Islamic legacy, nearly erasing Muslim influence within Azerbaijan. There has been an attempt to revive Islam in the aftermath of the U.S.S.R.'s collapse, but it has had only limited success.

More Azerbaijanis appear to be interested in redefining their newly independent national identity than in rediscovering their spiritual one.

Russia's rule over Azerbaijan not only prohibited the practice of Islam, it also suppressed national self-expression. During the last 200 years an Azerbaijani was either a subject of the czar or of the Communist rulers of the Soviet Union. Any attempts to demonstrate an independent Azerbaijani identity led to severe punishment. Many Azerbaijanis who tried to defy Russian authority were sent to labor camps or executed.

This forced integration went so far as to change Azerbaijan's alphabet from Arabic to Russian. The result has been linguistic chaos since 1991, when Azerbaijan became independent of Russian control. Some people would like to return to Arabic script, while others continue to interact in Russian. The situation is further complicated by the return of Western lettering, which had been banned for over half a century. Even though in 2001 Western, or Latin, script was decreed the official alphabet of Azerbaijan, old habits continue. Several Azerbaijani newspapers now combine the Arabic, Russian, and Western alphabets in their editions. It is also a common sight to see these three scripts on storefront signs advertising their merchandise. Such alphabetical rivalry well reflects the present discord that is taking place in Azerbaijan. This new country has yet to decide what type of culture it will develop.

Territorial Disputes

Another challenge facing Azerbaijan involves territory. The end of the Soviet Union led to a period of renewed ethnic tensions and rivalries. Foremost among these was the conflict between Azerbaijan and Armenia. Throughout history, there have always been tensions between the two societies. Primarily, these were due to religious differences, but the Soviet period made things worse. The Soviets redrew the boundaries of the two republics with little regard for either side's ancestral claims, and such insensitivity toward national awareness was bound to cause future problems. When Soviet power waned in the late 1980s,

Azerbaijan and Armenia decided that the time had come to resolve the situation.

The land in question, Nagorno-Karabakh, has traditionally been a source of ethnic friction. Azerbaijanis and Armenians equally assert that the area is part of their traditional homelands. What resulted was a bloody, emotional conflict in the early 1990s, which caused great territorial losses to Azerbaijan and turned many people into refugees. Avenging the defeat and humiliation suffered over Nagorno-Karabakh is a major issue among Azerbaijani nationalists, who suspect that Russia aided Armenia in determining the outcome.

A wrecked military vehicle rusts in a battlefield of the Askeran province, Nagorno-Karabakh, serving as a reminder of the bloody war fought over the territory in the 1990s. Nagorno-Karabakh is a fertile, mountainous area of 4,400 square kilometers in the southern Caucasus, situated inside the international border of Azerbaijan, yet most of the population is Armenian. A ceasefire negotiated in May 1994 ended the fighting, but the territorial dispute has never been resolved.

The Importance of Oil

In addition to Azerbaijan's strategic location, it possesses one of the world's largest oil **reserves**. Because the global demand for energy continues to grow, Azerbaijan assumes a very important role. Industry specialists think that much of Azerbaijan's oil lies untouched beneath the adjacent Caspian Sea. Once the Caspian's reserves are fully developed, it could potentially equal production from the nearby Persian Gulf, currently the world's major energy supplier.

Oil has played a central role throughout Azerbaijan's history. The nation supposedly derives its name from the Persian word for "fire" (*azer*), because there was an abundance of energy-derived geysers, which gushed throughout the landscape in ancient times. Baku, Azerbaijan's capital and largest city, was the world's first major oil-producing center in the early 20th century. Much of today's petroleum industry can trace its beginnings back to that period.

Azerbaijan's reputation faded when its energy production started to decline several decades ago. Technological advances, along with the Soviet Union's demise, have revitalized the nation's economy, creating the potential for a new oil bonanza. There is also increasing concern among industrialized nations that they have become too dependent on the Persian Gulf region for oil supplies. Considering that area's politically unstable environment, Azerbaijan emerges as a practical alternative.

Azerbaijan is a small but complex country. While cultural and historical aspects greatly define its national character, its place and potential importance in the world may be predetermined by its geography.

A satellite image shows the Caspian Sea. Because of its location on the world's largest inland body of water, Azerbaijan has access to vast deposits of oil and natural gas.

2

The Land

Azerbaijan is located on the eastern side of a region called Transcaucasia or the Transcaucasus. The countries of Georgia and Armenia are also part of this area. Transcaucasia is an *isthmus* and one of the world's most strategic places. The farthest reaches of Europe, Asia, and the Middle East meet here, their cultural and religious heritages predominating throughout the region.

With an area covering 33,428 square miles (86,600 sq. km), Azerbaijan is slightly smaller than the state of Maine. Russia borders it to the north, Georgia to the northwest, Armenia to the southwest, Iran to the south, and the Caspian Sea forms a natural border to the east. Nakhichevan, a small section of Azerbaijan that is geographically separated from the rest of the country by a 25-mile strip of Armenian territory, touches Turkey and the northwestern part of Iran. It is important to note that nearly one-fifth of Azerbaijan's territory was lost to Armenia in the early 1990s. This included the district of Nagorno-Karabakh, which had been governed by the Soviet republic of Azerbaijan since 1923.

Almost 8 million people live in Azerbaijan—the largest population of the Transcaucasian countries. A quarter of all Azerbaijanis reside in Baku. It is estimated that some 800,000 of Azerbaijan's inhabitants are refugees from the Nagorno-Karabakh dispute. Nearly all of these displaced people wish to return home when peace is restored.

Mountains and Lowlands

Roughly half of Azerbaijan's topography is mountainous. Only 15 percent of the land is considered suitable for farming. Except for the Caspian Sea, which is located on its eastern side, Azerbaijan is ringed by the Caucasus Mountains. The Caucasus are considered to be the formal point where the European continent ends and Asia begins. Two branches of this geographically important range are situated within Azerbaijan.

The Greater Caucasus range runs along Azerbaijan's northeastern border with Russia. While it contains Azerbaijan's highest peak, Mount Bazarduizi, which rises 14,652 feet (4,466 meters), the Greater Caucasus steeply descends southeastwards, toward the Caspian Sea. Mountain valleys and even forests dot the Greater Caucasus along this route, as do small villages and provincial towns. The southeast end of this range forms the Apsheron Peninsula, where the city of Baku is located. The Apsheron extends some 40 miles (65 km) into the Caspian, resembling an eagle's beak on maps and satellite photographs.

In the southwestern part of the nation, bordering Armenia, lies the Lesser Caucasus. This smaller mountain range averages approximately 10,000 feet (3,048 m) in height. The Lesser Caucasus winds through some politically critical environments, such as Armenia, the Nakhichevan region, and Nagorno-Karabakh. It also forms the southern border of Transcaucasia.

Glaciers cover the high mountains of the Greater Caucasus range. This range includes Azerbaijan's highest peak, Mount Bazarduizi.

At the southern end of the Lesser Caucasus are the Talysh Mountains. Although they are essentially a continuation of the Lesser Caucasus, the Talysh are situated within a completely different environment. The subtropical atmosphere in which these mountains are located noticeably contrasts the dry, semiarid conditions of the Lesser Caucasus. Nestled between the Talysh and the Caspian Sea is the Lenkoran lowland, where abundant rainfall allows the cultivation of tea, citrus, and fruit. It is also Azerbaijan's most productive agricultural region.

Between the Greater and Lesser Caucasus in central Azerbaijan is the Kura Depression. It is situated at the eastern end of an almost continuous lowland extending from the Black Sea in the west to the Caspian. In noted contrast to the Caucasus, much of the Kura Depression is below sea level. Pastoral activities dominate its semidesert-like hills and valleys.

A bus travels a narrow mountain road running through the Lesser Caucasus mountains.

Rivers and Lakes

There are over 1,250 rivers running through Azerbaijan, but no more than a handful are longer than 40 miles (65 km). Water runoffs from the Caucasus Mountains form the source for most of these rivers, eventually winding their way to the Caspian Sea. The majority of these rivers are not navigable.

There are two major rivers in Azerbaijan, the Kura and the Aras (also known as the Araxes). The Kura is the longest river in the Transcaucasus, flowing for 846 miles (1,364 km) from Turkey through Georgia and Azerbaijan before emptying into the Caspian. At its upper reaches near the Georgian capital of Tbilisi, the Kura runs through deep ravines and gorges. Below Tbilisi, the landscape changes to plains and lowlands, and the Kura is joined by several rivers, including the Araxes, that meander toward the

Caspian Sea. Just before it meets the Caspian coast, the Kura forms into a large delta.

Like the Kura, the 643-mile-long (1,060 km) Aras begins in eastern Turkey. Its route forms the southern border of Nakhichevan and part of Azerbaijan before connecting with the Kura. The Aras is symbolically important in Azerbaijani history, for in the early 19th century it served as the official boundary between the Muslim Persian and Christian Russian empires.

Azerbaijan's largest inland body of water is the Mingechaur Reservoir. Located near the Georgian border in northwestern Azerbaijan, the Mingechaur was created during the 1950s by damming the Kura River, which frequently flooded its lower course. The 234-square-mile (605 sq km) reservoir is Azerbaijan's major source of electric power.

The Caspian

Extending 744 miles (1,200 km) from north to south and with a width of 270 miles (434 km), the Caspian is the world's largest inland body of water. It covers an area roughly equal to the size of Japan, and is bounded by five countries—Russia, Iran, Kazakhstan, Turkmenistan, and Azerbaijan. The Caspian receives its name from a tribe that inhabited its shores in the fifth century B.C. Caviar production had been the Caspian's primary renown, until substantial amounts of oil were discovered below sea level.

Developing the Caspian's energy resources can make Azerbaijan a very wealthy nation, but it could also greatly harm the environment. The Caspian Sea has been damaged by ecological mismanagement. Raw sewage and agricultural pesticides have been dumped into its waters for years, greatly reducing the once-bountiful fishing and caviar industries. There are fears that oil leaking from planned underwater pipelines will turn the Caspian into a "dead" sea.

The Geography of Azerbaijan

Location: Southwestern Asia, bordering the Caspian Sea, between Iran and Russia, with a small European portion north of the Caucasus range

Area: (Slightly smaller than Maine)
> **Total:** 33,428 square miles (86,600 sq km)
> **Land:** 3,325 square miles (86100 sq km)
> **Water:** 193 square miles (500 sq km)

Borders: Armenia (with Azerbaijan—proper) 218 miles (566 km); Armenia (with Nakhichevan enclave) 85 miles (221 km); Georgia 124 miles (322 km); Iran (with Azerbaijan—proper) 167 miles (432 km); Iran (with Azerbaijan-Nakhichevan enclave) 69 miles (179 km); Russia 110 miles (284 km); Turkey 3 miles (9 km)

Climate: Mostly dry and semiarid with subtropical southeast Caspian coast

Terrain: Mountain ranges surrounding a central lowland, fertile southeastern coastal region

Elevation Extremes:

Lowest point: Caspian Sea—90 feet (28 meters) below sea level

Highest point: Mt. Bazarduizi—14,652 feet (4,466 meters)

Natural Hazards: Droughts

Source: Adapted from CIA World Factbook, 2004.

Is the Caspian even a sea? Some ***littoral*** countries, namely Russia and Iran, consider it an inland lake. According to maritime law, no country can exclusively claim the particular section of a lake it shares with other nations. Any potential projects must be shared or collectively agreed upon. There have been periodic meetings among the five Caspian states to resolve this issue. If the Caspian is ultimately judged to be a lake,

Azerbaijan could lose millions of dollars in selective contracts it has signed with international oil companies.

Climate

Azerbaijan's weather conditions vary considerably. The cold mountainous climate of the Greater Caucasus widely contrasts with the southeast's tropical humidity. Most of Azerbaijan, however, is dry or semiarid.

Precipitation is particularly uneven. The lowlands usually receive no more than 8 to 12 inches (20 to 31 centimeters) a year of rain, while the Greater Caucasus annually average between 39 to 51 inches (99 to 130 cm), mainly due to its slopes receiving large winter snowfalls. Some of the Greater Caucasus peaks remain snow-capped throughout the year. The Lenkoran lowland in the southeast receives excessive rainfalls that help make it Azerbaijan's most fertile region.

Most of Azerbaijan experiences hot and dry summers. The coastal region, however, can get very warm and humid. Baku's summer temperatures often reach 100° Fahrenheit (39° Celsius). Azerbaijan's winter weather is less varied, staying between 20° and 37° F (–7° to 3° C) throughout the nation.

During the cold seasons, Baku experiences very windy weather conditions. Hailing from Russia, these winds are known as "Baku northers," and can reach speeds exceeding 40 miles per hour. The name *Baku* is said to be derived from the Iranian words *bad khube* (bad winds).

Azerbaijan's prime minister, Ilham Aliyev, speaks at a press conference before the October 2003 presidential election. In that election voters chose Ilham to succeed his father Haidar Aliyev (whose portrait hangs behind Ilham) as president. However, critics claimed that the Aliyevs had subverted the democratic process and rigged the voting to ensure the outcome.

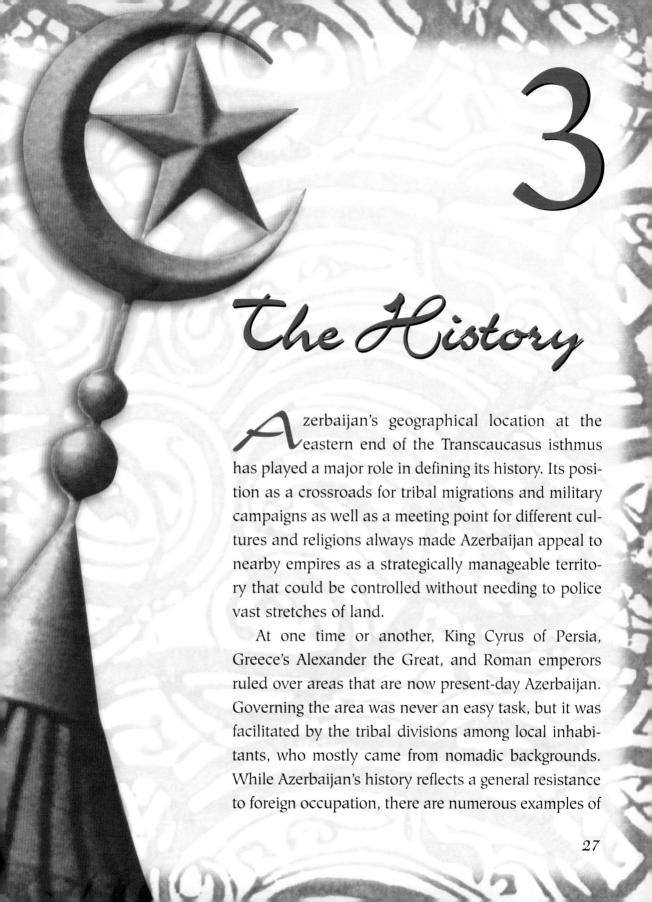

3

The History

zerbaijan's geographical location at the eastern end of the Transcaucasus isthmus has played a major role in defining its history. Its position as a crossroads for tribal migrations and military campaigns as well as a meeting point for different cultures and religions always made Azerbaijan appeal to nearby empires as a strategically manageable territory that could be controlled without needing to police vast stretches of land.

At one time or another, King Cyrus of Persia, Greece's Alexander the Great, and Roman emperors ruled over areas that are now present-day Azerbaijan. Governing the area was never an easy task, but it was facilitated by the tribal divisions among local inhabitants, who mostly came from nomadic backgrounds. While Azerbaijan's history reflects a general resistance to foreign occupation, there are numerous examples of princes and politicians conniving with occupying powers to suppress local dissent. This process of divide-and-rule has continued throughout Azerbaijan's history, often frustrating attempts to create a national identity. Although Azerbaijan is now an independent nation, factional squabbling persists.

Early History

The Scythians, a nomadic tribe that came westwards from Central Asia in the ninth century B.C., are Azerbaijan's earliest known settlers. A century later, another tribal group, the Medes, arrived from the south and drove the Scythians out of the area. Ethnically related to the Persians, the Medes established an empire that included southern Azerbaijan. In the sixth century B.C., the Medes and Persians united under the leadership of Cyrus the Great to conquer the mighty Assyrian Empire, which was based in

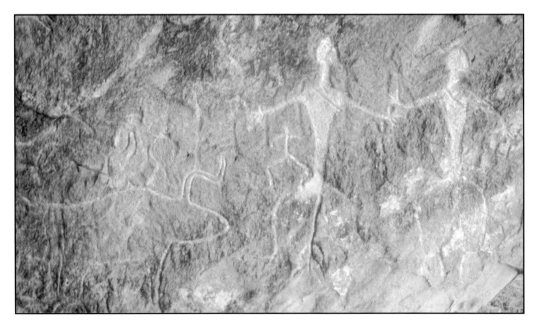

The 10,000-year-old Gobustan petroglyphs—some 3,500 inscriptions on 750 rocks south of Baku—are among the oldest surviving human records in the Caspian region.

> Legend has it that the name of the country, Azerbaijan, comes from the name of one of Alexander's satraps, Atropates, which means "protected by fire" in Persian. A former general under Alexander's command, Atropates supposedly lent his name to the particular region that he governed.

Mesopotamia. Assyria's defeat allowed the Medes and the Persians (also known as the Achaemenids) to take over western Azerbaijan.

Several centuries later, the Achaemenid Persians were defeated by the Macedonian conqueror Alexander the Great, who in 330 B.C. absorbed that empire into his holdings. Alexander left loyal Persian officials, called satraps, to administer the newly acquired domain as he advanced eastwards, toward India. Upon Alexander's death in 323 B.C., his empire gradually fragmented due to its unwieldy size and lack of a chosen successor.

Albania

The next major empire to rule Azerbaijan was the Roman Empire, between the first and third centuries A.D. It was during the Roman period that two states known as Albania and Aturpaken (or Atropaten) began to emerge. A number of historians believe that these nations, especially Albania, formed the roots of Azerbaijani statehood. It is uncertain whether the Albanians were an **indigenous** people or migrated from another area. Greek and Roman sources cite Albania as a large state with diverse economic activity, its own king, a separate language, and a considerable amount of autonomy. Particularly noteworthy was that Albania became a Christian state even under the rule of the then-pagan Romans.

The Christian missionaries Thomas and Andrew were said to have brought Christianity to Albania in the later stages of Roman rule. There was more tolerance toward Christians in Rome's outlying realms than within its heartlands. As long as Albania and other distant areas remained loyal to the empire, persecution toward such faiths would be limited.

It was a different situation with Rome's successors, the Persian Sasanian Empire. The Sasanians (also known as the Sassanids) took control over the region when a plague decimated the Roman legion guarding Albania in the second century A.D. Unable to maintain its military presence, Rome withdrew from Albania. The Sasanian kings adopted Zoroastrianism as their official religion, which caused a tense relationship with the Albanians.

The Sasanians were never able to completely control Albania. Although Albania was a **vassal** state, its kings frequently pursued their own agendas because Albania was too far from the Persian interior to be efficiently monitored by the Sasanians. Relations were additionally frayed by several Persian military campaigns against the Byzantine Empire, with which, as fellow Christians, Albanians sympathized. Albania frequently rebelled against its rulers, eventually winning back its independence when Sasanian power began to decline in the sixth century A.D. Albania's fight for sovereignty is a source of pride among many Azerbaijanis, who see it as a forerunner of the struggles they would face many centuries later.

The Introduction of Islam

In the seventh century A.D., the Arabs invaded the Transcaucasus, bringing with them their newly created Islamic faith. Islam eventually replaced Christianity and Zoroastrianism, becoming Azerbaijan's primary religion. Although other religious practices were tolerated under Islam, non-Muslims were heavily taxed by their Arab rulers. Religious conversion became the primary way out of this situation. Scholars believe that Christian Albania disappeared as a separate entity during the Arab reign, namely because its citizens chose to become Muslims.

Not everyone opted for Islam. In the ninth century, a non-Muslim religious sect known as the Khorramites challenged Arab supremacy. Its leader Babek started a popular revolt, known as the Babek Uprising, which included peasants as well as landed gentry who resented Arab control. In Azerbaijani folklore, Babek is the rough equivalent of France's Joan of Arc. The rebellion lasted 20 years and even drove the Arabs out of the Transcaucasus region for a short period of time. Arab forces regrouped, however, eventually defeating Babek, who was caught and executed.

Arrival of the Turks and the Seljuk Dynasty

Whereas the Arabs gave Azerbaijan its religious identity, a **Turkic** tribe shaped its cultural bearings. Azerbaijanis trace their heritage back to a federation of nomadic tribes known as the Oghuz Turks, who came from Central Asia in the eighth century A.D. Renowned for their fighting skills, the Oghuz

A Muslim-built minaret that dates from the mid-15th century dominates Baku's *Icheri Sehir* ("Inner City"). Islam arrived in the Transcaucasus region just decades after the Prophet Muhammad first publicly preached its tenets in Mecca during the early part of the seventh century.

were often recruited as mercenaries to fight in the Arab armies against the Byzantine Empire and other adversaries.

By the 10th century, the Oghuz had converted to Islam. They were attracted by the religion's philosophy that all Muslims were equal, regardless of origin or social standing. For tribal outsiders such as the Oghuz, this was a message that invited integration into other societies.

Participating in the mainstream led to societal changes. The Oghuz accumulated enough political clout to replace waning Arab control. This brought to power the Seljuk Dynasty, which lasted from the 11th to the 13th century.

The Seljuk period is renowned as something of a cultural golden age in Azerbaijan's history. The Oghuz were responsible for creating the Azerbaijani language, which is distinct from Persian and Arabic. Azerbaijani literature began rivaling works in Persian, which had been the predominant cultural language throughout the Muslim world. Several literary masterpieces were produced during this era, among them the writings of Nizami Ganjevi, whose poetry is revered in both Iran and Azerbaijan. The *Book of Dede Korkut*, an epic tale considered to be one of the most important works in Azerbaijani literature, details much of the Oghuz Turks' early lifestyle.

The Mongol Invasions

In the early 13th century, the Mongols swept into Azerbaijan. Unlike their Arab and Seljuk predecessors, who had introduced a new religion and culture, the Mongols wreaked havoc. They burned and looted whatever lay in their way, retreating back to their Central Asian homeland when finally exhausted.

One of these forays, toward the end of the 14th century, was led by the notorious Timur the Lame, or Tamerlane. Although he was ethnically Tatar (a member of a Turkic-speaking people who came from Siberia),

Tamerlane claimed that he was descended from the Mongols, who hailed from northern China, thereby uniting both ethnicities in campaigns of pillage and plunder. His late-14th-century incursion into the Caspian region was especially bloody, and nearly destroyed Azerbaijan. Tamerlane left no system of government in his wake, and after his death Azerbaijan went through a period of factional rule and deterioration.

In this void, governmental structures known as khanates gained strength. The word *khan* means "lord" in the Turkic language, and refers to the tribal allegiance between a leader and his followers. It had a different meaning in 15th-century Azerbaijan, when various regions began to rebound from the Mongol hordes and strong central authority was lacking. Khanates were the rough equivalents of city-states.

The concept actually had been created in the Sasanian period, when feudal lords were appointed as military governors for the far-flung Persian empire. One of the oldest and most prominent khanates was Shirvanshah, which became wealthy through its oil and salt trade. Petty and often quarreling **principalities** during dynastic periods, the khanates would nevertheless unite in helping Azerbaijan survive through such difficult times as the Mongol invasions. Unfortunately, these alliances were short-lived, and in peaceful times the khans would revert back to squabbling with each other.

Timur the Lame (known in the West as Tamerlane, 1336–1405) claimed to be descended from Genghis Khan. During his lifetime he conquered a huge area of territory that stretched across much of Central Asia. His armies were known for their brutality, and Timur looted the lands he conquered of their treasures, bringing them back to his capital city, Samarkand, where he built fabulous monuments and buildings. Because Timur never established an effective bureaucracy to govern the lands he conquered—fear of his armies kept the territories in line—his empire did not survive long after his death.

The Safavid Dynasty

By the 16th century, a new ruling dynasty known as the Safavids had emerged in Persia. The Safavids were Sufis, members of an unorthodox Islamic order that believed in religious mysticism. They also followed Shia Islam, the smaller of two major sects within the religion.

The division between the dominant Sunni Muslims and the minority Shiites had originated upon the death of Islam's founder, Muhammad, in 632 A.D. Because the Prophet left no appointed successor, two factions emerged to continue his legacy. One group believed that the leader of the Muslims should be selected based on his personal piety, and favored the prophet's companion Abu Bakr. They came to be known as the Sunnis, namely, "those who follow formal interpretations of Islam." A smaller group felt otherwise, believing that a relative of Muhammad should be the leader; they supported the claim of Ali, Muhammad's beloved cousin, as the Prophet's rightful heir. They became known as the Shiites. Although both Sunnis and Shiites follow the same basic teachings of Muhammad, each group has some different religious practices.

Shah Ismail I (ruled 1501–1524), the founder of the Safavid Dynasty, made Shiism a state religion, mainly for political reasons. The nearby Ottoman Turkish Empire presented a growing threat to Persia's traditional realms, which included Azerbaijan. Because the Ottomans were ethnically related to the Azerbaijanis and shared their Islamic beliefs, the Safavids needed something that would differentiate their rule or else risk losing an important part of their empire. Shah Ismail's strategy resulted in further defining Azerbaijan's identity. The vast majority of Azerbaijanis today are Shiite Muslims, a noticeable difference from their Turkic neighbors, most of whom are Sunni.

There was constant conflict between the Safavids and the Ottomans. The Ottomans controlled Azerbaijan for a brief period of time, until the

Safavids' most renowned leader, Shah Abbas I (1588–1629), reconquered the territory that had been lost. Inevitably, the constant warfare weakened Safavid administration, leading to its downfall in the early 18th century.

Russian Control

During the 18th century the encroachment of the Russian czars began to erode the power of the Safavid shahs. This was the start of a 200-year Russian presence that would greatly shape modern Azerbaijan. There were various reasons as to why the Russians began to look southwards, but Transcaucasia's strategic value became the main enticement. Emperor Peter the Great (1682–1725) made an initial foray into Persian-held territory during the early 1700s, but it was Empress Catherine the Great (1763–1799) who intensified Russia's involvement. By the end of her reign, the Christian states in Georgia and Armenia had allied with the Russian Empire.

Azerbaijan posed a more difficult problem for expansion. There were cultural and religious differences that Russia had not encountered with the Georgians and Armenians. Also, a new Persian dynasty, the Qajars, had replaced the Safavids; the Qajar rulers were determined to stop the encroaching Russians and assert Persian authority over the Transcaucasus. What ensued was called the Russian-Iranian Wars, and their outcomes would alter the regional balance of power.

Under the leadership of Catherine the Great, approximately 200,000 square miles of Central Asian territory was incorporated into the Russian empire.

Possessing superior armament, Russia defeated the Qajars in the First Russian-Iranian War (1804–1813). A peace accord, the Treaty of Gulistan, was signed in 1813, which made Persia cede control of any land it held or claimed north of the Aras River to the Russian Empire. The Qajars attempted to regain these territories in the Second Russian-Iranian War (1826–1828), but once again were decisively beaten. The Qajar ruler, Fath Ali Shah, sued for peace; this resulted in the Treaty of Turkmanchai (1828), which awarded Russia Nakhichevan and other western Azerbaijani khanates.

After the end of the Second Russian-Iranian War, the period of Russo-Persian rivalry officially came to an end in the Transcaucasus. With the Turkmanchai and Gulistan treaties, Persia acknowledged Russian domination over the region. The accords also divided Azerbaijan's population in half, with little if any regard for clan, tribal, or even family ties. Azerbaijanis thereupon would live in two vastly different societies, a separation which still exists today.

The Oil Boom

During the first decades of Russian rule, Azerbaijan was treated as little more than a distant colony. One Russian finance minister described it as an area "producing the raw materials of a southern climate." The major undertaking was to dismantle the khans and replace them with Czarist *gubernias* (provinces) and *oblasts* (regions).

The situation changed in 1872, when the oil sector was opened to the public. Petroleum had been a known product of Azerbaijan for many centuries, yet it had never been fully cultivated. Although technological breakthroughs had occurred, which would allow greater expansion, the Russian state maintained a monopoly over the extracting of oil, its refinement, and trade. Very few individuals were granted access to developing the precious commodity. Once this system was abolished, anyone who

This late 19th-century photograph shows numerous drilling rigs in an oil field at Baku, nicknamed the "forest of the Nobels."

could pay to probe Azerbaijan's plentiful oil fields was given a lease. An oil rush took place, sparking rapid industrial growth throughout the region.

Baku was the center of this oil bonanza. Its location on the oil-rich Apsheron Peninsula turned the small town into one of the world's first petroleum centers. During the last half of the 19th century, Baku grew from 14,000 inhabitants to 206,000, which made it the largest city in Transcaucasia. It also possessed an excellent harbor on the Caspian Sea, an important factor in shipping oil and related products to European markets via Russia. This was the primary means of transport until the Transcaucasian Railway was built in the mid-1880s, connecting Baku to the Black Sea for quicker routing westwards.

An excellent book about the oil-boom period in Azerbaijan is *Blood and Oil*, by a writer who used the pen name Essad Bey. He relates his experiences as the son of a wealthy oil magnate during the late 19th to early 20th centuries. In one passage, he describes what Baku was like before the oil rush:

> Forty years ago Baku was a desert city. There was not yet a single street that could be considered European. Not a single tree sheltered the inhabitants from the burning heat. The whole place consisted of a few clay huts and a few barbaric places, which were built on the desert sand and surrounded by a single wall. The thick walls of the palace afforded but slight shelter against the sun. There were no rippling fountains, which every other house in the Orient possesses. Water had to be brought in sacks from a distance and hardly sufficed for drinking and washing. When the heat became unbearable, the wealthy people left their houses and went to the seashore where one could pretend it was cooler.

—Essad Bey, *Blood and Oil*, page 11.

The rapid growth of the oil industry changed Baku into a boomtown. Its lawless atmosphere resembled America's Western frontier. Young men came to Baku in search of fortune and adventure; over two-thirds of its population was under the age of 30. Oil rigs proliferated throughout the area, even in places that were considered unproductive or risky.

One of the most prominent families who invested in Baku's oilfields was the Nobels. Although they are better known for having established the prizes in various fields of research which bear their name, the Nobels' wealth was created in the oil business. It was Robert Nobel, brother of the more famous Alfred, who arrived at the start of Baku's oil boom and bought a refinery, which would rapidly expand into one of the world's major oil companies by the beginning of the 20th century. The Nobel Company exported more oil than all other Baku firms combined, and was responsible for massive construction projects throughout the city.

Other investors followed the Nobels, particularly the Rothschild family, which was based in Paris. Their Caspian-Black Sea Society for Commerce and Industry rivaled the Nobels' operations. Together they came to symbolize the West for Baku, bringing new technological and business innovations to the region. Despite the dominance these "giants" had in the oil industry, other companies also profited. Besides the Nobels and the Rothschilds, there were several British, French, Belgian, German, and Greek firms operating there. By the 1890s, Baku was practically an international city.

Social Tensions

Baku's oil boom promised wealth, but it also sowed the seeds of discontent and resentment. There was an influx of Russian settlers, which started to affect Azerbaijan's social structure. Most of the oilfields were purchased by Russians and the local Armenian population, who formed the administrative elite within that industry. Although there were some noticeable exceptions, the vast majority of Azerbaijani Turks worked as laborers for meager pay.

Baku symbolized this ethnic schism. It may have been a multinational center, but it was no melting pot. Ethnic communities lived in their own distinct neighborhoods, hardly interacting with each other. Most Azerbaijani Turks could live in their particular *mahalle*, or neighborhood, and do their daily chores without having to encounter foreigners. The Russians, on the other hand, did little to integrate Azerbaijanis into their own business or civic networks.

Conditions were less stringent outside Baku. The foreign presence was less noticeable, and more Azerbaijanis engaged in local administration. As a result, the civil service became a primary channel for adopting European habits, which would become an important factor in the foreseeable future.

The Tatar-Armenian War

By the beginning of the 20th century, Baku's oil boom started to decline. An economic depression occurred, which left many oil workers unemployed and without any means of support. Baku's reputation as a boomtown started to change to that of a city bursting with labor unrest. There were general strikes, which eventually led to the signing of the first labor contract with Russia. However, it failed to solve Azerbaijan's ethnic tensions.

The already profound antagonisms between Azerbaijani Turks and the Armenian community grew deeper. Both groups were suspicious of each other for several reasons. Foremost was the Azerbaijani sense that the Armenians acted as Russia's colonial agents. Christian Armenia regarded Russia as its protector from Muslim rule. After the Russian-Iranian wars, many Armenians moved into the areas that the Gulistan and Turkmanchai treaties had ceded to Moscow. Many Azerbaijani Turks felt that the Russians gave preferential treatment to these newly arrived Armenians, who were better educated and more adept at dealing with the business side of the oil boom. The vast majority of Baku's oil leases were owned by Armenian investors. Azerbaijani Turks began to feel like second-class citizens within their own homeland.

The simmering discontent turned into communal violence that raged from 1905 to 1907. Both populations suffered thousands of casualties, and there was significant property damage. This conflict was labeled the Tatar-Armenian War ("Tatar" was the popular term used by Czarist Russia to describe all Muslim nationalities under its rule), and was the opening chapter of what would become the tumultuous nature of Armenian-Azerbaijani relations.

New Concepts

The early 1900s were a time of upheavals all over the Transcaucasian region. Along with the industrial growth that was transforming Azerbaijan came new ideas. Several ideologies were introduced, which would shape the country's politics for many years. Russia experienced severe unrest, as did neighboring Iran and the Ottoman Empire. The citizens of these nations wanted to end the all-powerful authority of the czars, shahs, and sultans, replacing it with greater public participation. Different philosophies evolved as to what would be the best forms of government.

Azerbaijan became a meeting point for these theories. European notions, such as Socialism and Liberal thought, became predominant in Armenian and other non-Muslim communities. Azerbaijani Turks were drawn to other ideas, namely pan-Turkism and pan-Islamism. Pan-Turkism promoted cultural unity and cooperation among the world's Turkic people. Its followers envisioned the Ottoman Empire uniting with Azerbaijan and other Turkic people throughout Central Asia to form one giant entity. This would become a major strategy for Ottoman forces when they battled Russia and its allies during World War I (1914–1918).

Pan-Islamism was a more inclusive movement, which looked to bring together all Muslims, regardless of their ethnic, national, or **sectarian** differences. It was much more international in its outlook than pan-Turkism's regional concentration. While pan-Islamism did not reject Western techniques and methods, European colonialism was considered the primary foe. Many Azerbaijanis who supported this concept felt that the Russian occupation had cut them off from communicating with the Islamic world.

The movement that best embraced these sentiments was the Musavat (Equality) Party. Formed just before the start of World War I, Musavat would eventually become the largest political force within Azerbaijan. It advocated Muslim unity and independence, a popular message throughout all sectors of Azerbaijani society. In due time, its officials would emerge as Azerbaijan's leading statesmen.

World War I and Its Aftermath

The first few years of World War I, which began in the summer of 1914, had a minimal impact on Azerbaijan. Czar Nicholas II had exempted his Muslim subjects from military conscription, fearing their loyalty in fighting against his Ottoman opponents. Ironically, this policy would set the stage for much bloodshed, as the closing stages of World War I spun Azerbaijan into major upheaval. In a three-year period (1917–1920), the nation would experience a collapsed empire, revolutionary turmoil, brief independence, and Russian reoccupation. What began as an era of anxious hope ended in frustration and disappointment.

When Nicholas II was overthrown in 1917, a huge governmental void occurred. There was pandemonium throughout the Russian Empire, particularly in the Transcaucasus. Because Georgia and Armenia were Christian societies, the czar had recruited men from those areas to fight the Ottomans, thus arming and enabling them to assert their independence after the monarchy had been toppled.

The unarmed Azerbaijanis were at a comparative disadvantage. If they were to be on equal standing with the Georgians and Armenians, they needed weapons, quickly. Otherwise, Azerbaijan would be seized and divided among its neighbors.

Deserting Russian soldiers became the primary source for arming Azerbaijanis. This particularly alarmed the Armenians, who hadn't forgotten the Tatar-Armenian War a decade earlier; it also alarmed the Bolsheviks, who were fighting for control of Russia and were fearful of a militarized Muslim entity within their realm. Amid such concerns, around the region Azerbaijani militias began to form.

Baku was particularly tense. The local government, which had taken on greater importance in the absence of a strong Russian presence, was mainly administered by members of the city's Armenian community. In early 1918, Baku's authorities, who were called the *soviet* (the Russian word for "council"), ordered Muslim militias to disarm within the city's boundaries. Baku's Muslim population refused, fearing that they would be defenseless while Armenians and Russians were allowed to retain their own armed forces. Attempts to negotiate failed, and resulted in a conflict in which the better-armed Armenians and Russians prevailed. A massacre followed, in which an estimated 3,000 Muslims were killed and many more fled in terror. Azerbaijanis refer to this incident as the March Days of 1918, regarding it as a solemn chapter in their struggle for nationhood.

A large crowd assembles in Red Square to hear Bolshevik leaders Joseph Stalin and Leon Trotsky (standing on podium in the center), October 1917. The success of the Bolshevik revolution resulted in the establishment of the Soviet Union.

Short-lived Independence

Azerbaijan would finally achieve freedom, although it was only for a brief period of time. The czar's downfall created an administrative vacuum throughout the Transcaucasus. The region was affected by the Russian Revolution's turbulent state of affairs and conflicts between the Bolshevik successors and their various adversaries. This unrest was favorable to the Ottoman Empire, which perceived neighboring Russia's turmoil as an excellent opportunity to ally with their Turkic brethren and to expand their sovereignty to post-czarist Azerbaijan and Central Asia, thus promoting their goal of pan-Turkism.

Reeling from the March Days calamity, Azerbaijani Muslims gratefully welcomed support for their nationalist aspirations. A treaty of friendship was consequently signed between Azerbaijani leaders and the Ottoman Empire, which guaranteed the latter's assistance in surmounting Armenian and Russian advantages. A joint Ottoman-Azerbaijani army was formed; it seized Baku in September 1918.

It was during the six-month period between the March Days and Baku's capture that Azerbaijan declared its independence. The Azerbaijani Democratic Republic was history's first self-governing Muslim democracy, yet its survival essentially depended on outside support. Although the Ottomans (whose own citizens would establish the Republic of Turkey, the world's second Muslim republic, in 1923) would have preferred Azerbaijan to be part of their empire, they backed the proclamation nonetheless.

World War I ended in the fall of 1918, and the defeated Ottomans ceded their influence within Azerbaijan to the victorious Allies. One of the Allied powers, the British Empire, became Azerbaijan's new guardian. Britain's presence ensured that Azerbaijan's oilfields and railways were protected from Russian Bolshevik sabotage or armed incursions. The British opposed the Bolsheviks ideologically because of Bolshevik support of communism, a philosophy that advocated that all societies needed to be changed by world revolution of the working classes.

The antipathy was illustrated by what happened to members of Baku's *soviet*. When fleeing from Ottoman control, these Bolshevik officials, who were called **commissars**, were eventually captured by British forces in Central Asia. Although Russia and Great Britain had been on the same side during World War I, in 1918 the Bolsheviks decided they would not continue Russian involvement in the conflict and consequently withdrew from the war. The British viewed this as a betrayal of their alliance and held little sympathy for their captives' plight. Twenty-six commissars were summarily shot, their executions energizing the Bolshevik cause and becoming a part of Communist legend.

Although the Musavat Party became the dominant political force in the Azerbaijani Democratic Republic, it was never able to govern by itself. Coalition cabinets became a standard feature; five new governments were formed during the nation's two-year existence from 1918 to 1920. Musavat's one-third share of the legislative seats in the Democratic Republic's parliament was not enough to effectively set programs and policies. It competed with eight other parties of varying philosophies that were more adept at provoking crisis than crafting laws.

The British withdrew from Azerbaijan in the late summer of 1919, primarily due to finalized peace agreements and budgetary problems. Their withdrawal left the nation without a guardian that would protect it from Russian claims. Eight months after Britain had left Azerbaijan, the Bolsheviks orchestrated a coup that toppled the Azerbaijani Democratic Republic. On April 27, 1920, Azerbaijan was proclaimed a Soviet Socialist Republic.

The Communist Era

Communism in Azerbaijan was defined by cultural suppression and total economic control. Azerbaijani nationalism was to be eradicated and replaced by anonymous citizenship in the newly created Soviet Union. The Communist authorities wanted to dispel the past and form a completely new society.

One of Communism's primary targets was the alphabet. The Arabic script, which had been used there for centuries, was declared obsolete by the Communist authorities, who favored developing a Latin version. "Latinization" was also a way to stop future generations of Azerbaijanis from reading pre-Soviet literature that might promote notions of freedom and ethnicity. Based on this logic, Azerbaijan changed to Latin lettering in 1924. However, the attempt to prevent reading of anti-Soviet writings was unsuccessful. Turkey, which had also changed to the Latin script during the 1920s, had become the primary location for Azerbaijani exiles to

Russian tractors harvest grain on the Ordzhonikidze state farm in Azerbaijan. Under the communist system, the Soviet government assumed ownership of all farms, businesses, factories, and other private property in Russia and the republics.

express their thoughts and ideas about the Soviet regime. In response, a decade later the Communists disavowed Latin in favor of Russian Cyrillic, a harder script to convey and interpret in Western societies. The Cyrillic alphabet remained the basis for writing in Azerbaijan and the other Central Asian republics until the Soviet Union's demise.

Another major aim for the Communists was seizing privately owned property and placing it under state authority. This was called nationalization, and those businessmen and farmers who refused to cooperate were severely punished. All businesses and even personal valuables were "requisitioned" without compensation, for unspecified economic programs. What amounted to robbing the public of their private possessions was another form of societal control, primarily meant to erase class and commercial differences within Azerbaijani society.

Combating nationalist sentiments was an issue for Communist authorities not only in Azerbaijan, but throughout the Transcaucasus. Armenia and Georgia were also independent states until the Russian Communists ousted their governments after World War I. They faced the same situations and dilemmas as Azerbaijan did. The Communists decided that the best way to rid these three societies of their respective nationalism was to group them together into one regional entity. The result was the Transcaucasian Soviet Federated Socialist Republic, which became part of the Union of Soviet Socialist Republics (U.S.S.R.) in 1922. The Transcaucasian Republic existed until 1936, when the Soviet leader Joseph Stalin declared that the nationalist issue had been solved and replaced by "proletarian internationalism." Azerbaijan, Armenia, and Georgia subsequently became separate republics of the U.S.S.R.

The Great Terror and World War II

Exile, imprisonment, and executions were a part of life during Azerbaijan's early Communist years. From the country's **Sovietization** until

World War II, the nation experienced what historians have called the "Great Terror." This was a movement intended to strengthen the government's power throughout the Soviet Union. Any person who questioned—or was even suspected of doubting—the righteousness of the Communist rule was arrested and usually executed as "an enemy of the state." Landowners, merchants, writers, and artists were particularly targeted. Mosques were closed and religious leaders forced to conform with Soviet principles.

This campaign, directed by Joseph Stalin, afflicted all of the Soviet Union's republics, but it particularly devastated Azerbaijan. A connection to the Musavat or other non-Communist political parties was an automatic death sentence. Although the total number of Azerbaijani victims of the Great Terror is unknown, it is estimated that during its severest years—1937 and 1938—some 120,000 citizens perished. The terror affected Azerbaijan's culture and all levels of society.

The Soviet purges ended when Germany invaded the Soviet Union in 1941, drawing the U.S.S.R. into World War II (1939–1945). Baku's plentiful oil supply was a major objective for Germany; Nazi leader Adolf Hitler believed that gaining control of this resource could ensure a German victory. Although the Nazis reached the northern ridge of the Greater Caucasus, they were unable to conquer Azerbaijan and accomplish their goal.

Baku's petroleum played a critical role in the Soviet war effort. Seventy percent of the military's oil provisions came from Azerbaijan. The oil fields were considered so vital to the outcome of World War II that the Allies made plans to bomb the oil fields if Germany seized them.

Azerbaijan also made a substantial contribution to the Soviet war effort in terms of military personnel during World War II. Nearly half a million Azerbaijanis went to war, with 30,000 earning decorations for bravery. Soviet propaganda appealed to Azerbaijan's national sentiments, evoking the legends of Babek and of the khanates' resistance to foreign invaders.

German soldiers cross a semi-covered tank trap in the Caucasus, September 1942. The Baku oil fields were the ultimate target for the Nazi invasion of the U.S.S.R., but Hitler's plan to seize the valuable territory was thwarted at Stalingrad, several hundred miles north of Azerbaijan.

Several thousand Azerbaijanis who hated the Soviet system defected to the German side. Along with other defectors from Soviet rule who wanted to establish their own independent homelands, they fought for the Nazis against the Soviet army. After Germany's surrender in May 1945, many of these soldiers were caught and imprisoned or executed.

Postwar Years

Azerbaijan came out of World War II in an exhausted state. The war's demands had nearly drained the nation's oil capacity, and when new quantities were discovered in Russia's Siberian provinces during the 1950s, the Caspian region's economic importance began to fade. Between 1940 and 1960, Azerbaijan's share in total Soviet oil production fell from 71 percent to 12 percent.

Although it had been in the Soviet interest to encourage nationalist sentiments during the war, that abruptly ended when the war did. A new campaign was launched to suppress such notions, with emphasis placed on Russia as an "older brother" who would help Azerbaijan regain its economic importance. This was an empty promise; the Caspian oil fields gradually fell into disrepair amid corruption and inept leadership.

Azerbaijan's environment continued to decline until the late 1960s, when the republic's new Communist Party leader, Haidar Aliyev, took over. Unlike his predecessors, Aliyev sought to clean up governmental fraud and improve Azerbaijan's economy. As a former official in the KGB, the Soviet Union's state security organization, he knew how to threaten and intimidate subordinates to achieve these goals. Aliyev's most noticeable accomplishment, however, was changing the ethnic composition of Azerbaijan's Communist Party system. There had been few Azerbaijani Turkish officials managing the nation's infrastructure. Russians and Armenians had controlled the important administrative positions since the Communist period began, reluctant to promote anyone who was not of their own nationality. Aliyev ended this practice. He appointed Azerbaijani Turks to high positions, which produced a new elite more representative of the republic's population.

When he took over leadership of the Soviet republic of Azerbaijan, Haidar Aliyev attacked official corruption, took steps to improve the economy, and brought Turkic Azerbaijanis into higher levels of government.

The Soviet leadership was impressed by Haidar Aliyev's performance, promoting him to be a member of the Politburo, the Communist Party's executive legislature, in 1982. Although he went to Moscow as a senior Soviet official, Aliyev would inevitably return to Azerbaijan under different circumstances and in a completely new capacity.

Communist society underwent major changes during the 1980s. An era of reform was ushered in by Mikhail Gorbachev, who in 1985 had been selected to lead the U.S.S.R. Gorbachev believed in a more open and tolerant environment throughout the Soviet Union, where people could freely express their thoughts without facing grave consequences. Additionally government would become more answerable to public concerns. This campaign became popularly known as *glasnost* (openness) and *perestroika* (restructuring).

Azerbaijan was profoundly affected by these new measures. Throughout the Azerbaijani population, age-old grievances that had been fiercely suppressed came to the surface. It was generally felt that greater public involvement could solve these matters and create a better future.

Azerbaijanis particularly focused upon two topics—the decaying oil industry and a major dispute with Armenia over who controlled the Nagorno-Karabakh region. Whereas the petroleum issue concentrated upon the better management of Azerbaijan's natural resources, Nagorno-Karabakh quickly became an emotionally pressing issue.

Nagorno-Karabakh

Due to its precarious location between Armenia and Azerbaijan, the Nagorno-Karabakh issue has always been very complex. The population of this mountainous and barely accessible enclave is predominantly Armenian, but its commercial and historic ties arguably veer toward Azerbaijan. It was once part of an Azerbaijani khanate, and major transportation links originate eastwards from the Caspian region rather than toward the western-situated Black Sea.

In the early stages of Soviet rule, Nagorno-Karabakh became administratively connected to Azerbaijan. The decision was made after a series of contentious debates between Armenia and Azerbaijan over who rightfully claimed the territory. It was finally determined that a certain degree of autonomy, or self-government, for Nagorno-Karabakh was the best solution. Although the region's finances were to be controlled by Azerbaijani authorities, Nagorno-Karabakh could establish its own legislative assembly. This solution gave Nagorno-Karabakh the status of an autonomous oblast, or district, within the overall U.S.S.R. governmental structure.

The arrangement continued without major controversy until *glasnost* and *perestroika* were introduced. Armenia saw the new policy as an opportunity to make Nagorno-Karabakh a part of their republic. It was argued that Azerbaijan discriminated against Armenians by economically neglecting the oblast. Petitions advocating unification gave way to demonstrations throughout Armenia and Nagorno-Karabakh. Violence inevitably occurred, and, by the late 1980s, communal strife similar to the Tatar-Armenian War 80 years before was underway.

Within Azerbaijan, the new atmosphere of *glasnost* allowed the emergence of several non-Communist associations. The largest one was the Popular Front, which was founded in 1989. Although the Popular Front encompassed a wide cross-section of Azerbaijani society, its leadership mostly came from academic ranks. As was the case with similar movements across the Soviet Union at that time, these individuals comprised a generation that had not personally experienced the Great Terror, and therefore advocated change without fear of potential consequences. It is also worth noting that the Popular Front never used Islamic themes or rhetoric to mobilize its supporters. Despite being concerned about Christian Armenia's intentions regarding Nagorno-Karabakh, the Popular Front practiced **secular** politics.

The Popular Front also advocated major changes regarding

Soviet peacekeeping troops mingle with civilians in the disputed Nagorno-Karabakh enclave, October 1989.

Azerbaijan's relationship within the Soviet Union. Among its goals were gaining control over its energy resources, the ability to veto various laws imposed by Moscow, and even the right to secede from the Soviet Union. As the situation deteriorated in Nagorno-Karabakh, the Popular Front was able to exercise greater influence on Azerbaijan's Communist Party, a development that would have been impossible before *glasnost*.

Black January

The wrangling between Armenia and Azerbaijan intensified in late 1989. Armenian leadership declared Nagorno-Karabakh part of their republic without notifying the Soviet leadership of their intentions. Gorbachev condemned Armenia's attempt to annex the troubled region as a violation of Azerbaijan's sovereignty, but it had little effect.

Riots broke out in Baku after Armenia's announcement. The city's Armenian community was attacked, which resulted in considerable bloodshed. Matters were spinning out of control, and in January 1990 Soviet authorities sent troops to Baku so that stability could be restored.

But the supposedly peacekeeping purpose of this operation changed as things progressed. The growing power of the Popular Front threatened the Communist Party's dominance throughout the U.S.S.R. If such an organization existed in Azerbaijan, it could spread to other Soviet republics, bringing Communism's preeminent position into question. Although *glasnost* and *perestroika* permitted reforming the Soviet system, any challenge to its foundations was rejected.

From the Communist viewpoint, the Popular Front posed a greater threat than Nagorno-Karabakh. The "peacekeeping" Soviet troops arrested Popular Front officials and shut down their headquarters. Hundreds of Azerbaijanis who protested against what was happening were either shot or imprisoned. The heavy-handed response made Azerbaijani public opinion turn solidly against the Communist Party and the Soviet Union. While this event is referred to as Black January, it also indicated that the U.S.S.R. was in deep trouble, and that the system was incapable of any genuine changes.

By the end of 1991, the Soviet Union would cease to exist. The U.S.S.R. splintered into separate independent republics, each faced with its own list of hopes and problems.

The Second Independent Republic

On August 30, 1991, the independent Republic of Azerbaijan was established. For Azerbaijan, freedom was not a new concept, but the new country hardly benefited from its 1918–20 experience. Within the first few years of its existence, the republic would see three presidents, two governments—both forced from power—and innumerable attempts to overthrow the presiding authority. The reasons behind most of this turmoil revolved around Nagorno-Karabakh and a revived interest in Azerbaijan's oil riches.

The Nagorno-Karabakh situation would prove to be particularly vexing. Following the Soviet Union's downfall, the controversy had descended into armed conflict between the newly independent states of Azerbaijan and Armenia. To preempt an Armenian takeover, Azerbaijan ended Nagorno-Karabakh's Soviet-era autonomy, making it an integral part of the republic's territory. In reply, the Armenian-dominated Nagorno-Karabakh legislature declared its own independence. Armenia refrained from recognizing Nagorno-Karabakh's independence, but nonetheless lent its support to ridding that specific area of all Azerbaijani presence.

This essentially amounted to ethnic cleansing, creating for Azerbaijan a serious refugee problem that still exists today. During the course of this purification campaign, Azerbaijani civilians were massacred in the town of Khojaly. The incident shocked Azerbaijan, intensifying hatred and a need for revenge.

Khojaly would also cause the downfall of the republic's first government, which was led by Ayaz Mutalibov, who had previously headed Azerbaijan's Communist Party. Azerbaijanis blamed Mutalibov for their country's weak response to Armenia's aggression and for its failure to protect his nation's citizenry. He was succeeded by Abufaz Elchibey, the leader of the Popular Front, in June 1992. The democratically elected Elchibey was a historian who had been imprisoned during the Soviet period for his nationalist views. Although he clearly communicated Azerbaijan's aspirations and concerns, Elchibey lacked any governmental experience, which became a liability in his position as a leader of independent Azerbaijan.

Elchibey pursued an ambitious agenda. Besides continuing the struggle with Armenia over Nagorno-Karabakh, Elchibey began to steer Azerbaijan away from its close relationship with Russia. He invited

Western companies to explore Azerbaijan's offshore oil deposits in the Caspian Sea, a market that had been ignored during the Soviet era. This policy displeased the Russians, who felt Elchibey was allowing foreigners into what had been their sphere of influence for hundreds of years.

Russia retaliated by providing military assistance to Armenia in the Nagorno-Karabakh conflict. As a result, Azerbaijan was unable to recover its territorial losses from the better-equipped Armenians. One-fifth of Azerbaijan's territory fell into Armenia's hands during the Elchibey period, and the number of refugees swelled to nearly a million people.

A mutiny broke out among Azerbaijan's military over Elchibey's handling of the Nagorno-Karabakh situation. It escalated into a full-scale revolt that forced him to flee Baku in June 1993. A referendum vote was

An Azerbaijani soldier mans a heavy machine gun at a front-line position in the war over Nagorno-Karabakh, 1992. Armenia's success in the war, which many suspected was due to Russian assistance, led to the collapse of Azerbaijan's Elchibey government and the return of Haidar Aliyev as president.

held shortly thereafter, which judged Elchibey's performance to be unsatisfactory. Amid Armenian concerns, Russian intrigues, and oil's allure, Azerbaijan needed a strong, seasoned leader.

Aliyev's Return

Many people believed the best candidate to fulfill Azerbaijan's governmental requirements was Haidar Aliyev. Although he was 70 years old and considered by some a relic of the Communist era, Aliyev possessed the necessary experience for dealing with Azerbaijan's difficulties. He was easily elected to lead the nation in the aftermath of Elchibey's rule.

Aliyev successfully stabilized Azerbaijan. This was essentially achieved in a resolute manner, with little tolerance for dissent. Such groups as the Popular Front continued to operate, but their influence was largely curtailed by strict rules and regulations.

Shortly after taking office, Aliyev negotiated a ceasefire agreement that ended the fighting over Nagorno-Karabakh. Although a political solution has yet to be found, the truce ended the violence and permitted Azerbaijan to redirect attention toward developing its offshore energy potential.

In 1994, an agreement was signed with a group of international oil corporations to explore the Caspian Sea's bountiful reserves of oil and natural gas. This deal is popularly referred to as "the contract of the century," and has resulted in extensive foreign investment for Azerbaijan. Reviving Azerbaijan's oil productivity enabled the nation to achieve a fair degree of independence from Russian influence. Consequently, Aliyev became the target of several plots that were intended to destabilize his authority.

The vast majority of Azerbaijanis saw Aliyev as a savior who rescued their fledgling nation from uncertainty and had given it a hopeful future. He successfully managed Azerbaijan's post-Soviet transition, yet seemed unable to relinquish certain Communist traits. Election results were always questioned during the Aliyev period, particularly because he

Azerbaijani supporters of defeated presidential candidate Isa Gambar fight with police in downtown Baku, October 2003, protesting the results of the allegedly rigged election won by Ilham Aliyev.

always won 75 percent of all the cast votes. Political opponents as well as international organizations charged Aliyev with inflating results to justify his authoritarian ways, and claimed that Azerbaijan's electoral process was a travesty.

Haidar Aliyev died in December 2003 at the age of 80, after a prolonged illness. During his final months, Aliyev created a controversy by designating his son Ilham to succeed him before a national election in October 2003. Aliyev's critics accused him of creating a dynasty that subverted the democratic process, and there was heated debate over Ilham's suitability to lead Azerbaijan. As president of SOCAR, Azerbaijan's state oil company, Ilham possessed a managerial background but no political experience.

Ilham easily won the October 2003 election, albeit with numerous questions about its legitimacy. The Popular Front and other opposition parties have charged that there was massive ballot fraud, prompting sizeable demonstrations throughout Azerbaijan. The clamor has subsided for now, but it remains to be seen whether Ilham Aliyev can successfully continue his father's legacy.

Azerbaijani workers prepare pumping equipment during their shift near the tower at an oil field near Baku. Azerbaijan controls vast untapped reserves of oil under the Caspian Sea, and the development of these fields should pump billions of dollars into the country's economy.

The Economy, Politics, and Religion

Although it is the least industrially developed of the Transcaucasian republics, Azerbaijan's future appears to be much brighter than its neighbors. The primary reason for such optimism is the nation's energy resources. However, in order to fulfill its potential, Azerbaijan must meet a number of challenges.

After the U.S.S.R. collapsed, Azerbaijan experienced profound shock. The Azerbaijani economy was tightly bound to the Soviet system and consisted of primarily trading products with Russia and other republics. Lacking these familiar outlets, during the early years of independence Azerbaijan's commercial activity decreased by 60 percent.

While Azerbaijan wanted to be free from Russian economic control, this freedom would come at a severe price. High inflation eroded Azerbaijani incomes, leading to widespread poverty. Prices were increasing at an average of 50 percent each month, creating an expansive black market for everyday items. The Nagorno-Karabakh crisis further worsened matters.

Realizing that Russia's markedly weakened currency (the ruble) was negatively impacting its economy, Azerbaijan established its own currency. The manat began circulating in 1992, and this slowly began to stabilize the economic situation. Azerbaijan's inflation problems dramatically declined from 1,664 percent in 1994 to 85 percent in 1995. The nation's business climate began to noticeably improve. Aided by a stabilizing political situation and the "contract of the century," Azerbaijan began to shift from its Soviet-era bearings.

Oil and Gas

The signing of the 1994 "contract of the century" ignited a spending spree in Azerbaijan's energy sector. Eight other contracts quickly followed, for different oilfields off Azerbaijan's Caspian coast. The nation has already signed deals worth more than $40 billion, with little sign of an investment slowdown. Various predictions abound that this new oil rush will exceed $60 billion, resulting in a $100 billion profit over the next three decades. An estimated 620 to 730 million tons of untapped oil lies offshore, an amount that can sufficiently lessen the West's dependency on Persian Gulf reserves.

The usual terms of an oil contract are reflected in the 1994 contract agreement. A **consortium** of foreign oil companies (there were seven in the original 1994 deal) will develop a particular oilfield, usually over a 30-year period. For the first decade, Azerbaijan will only keep a third of the profits, while the rest goes to cover the investors' operating costs. By 2005,

The Economy of Azerbaijan

Gross Domestic Product (GDP): $26.34 billion

GDP per capita: $3,400

Inflation: 2.9%

Natural Resources: petroleum, natural gas, iron ore, zinc, marble, limestone

Industry (46% of GDP): petroleum and natural gas, petroleum products, oilfield equipment, steel, iron ore, cement, chemicals and petrochemicals, textiles

Agriculture: (14% of GDP): cotton, grain, rice, grapes, fruit, vegetables, tea, tobacco, livestock (cattle, pigs, sheep, goats)

Services: (40% of GDP): government, banking, tourism

Foreign Trade:

  Imports: $2.5 billion—machinery and equipment, oil products, foodstuffs, metals, chemicals

  Exports: $2.6 billion—oil and gas, machinery, cotton, foodstuffs

Currency Exchange Rate: 4,912 Azerbaijani manat = US $1 (2004)

*GDP is the total value of goods and services produced in a year.

All figures are 2003 estimates unless otherwise noted.

Source: CIA World Factbook, 2004; bloomberg.com.

the field is expected to be fully operable, and Azerbaijan's earnings share will increase to five-sixths for the next 20 years. These arrangements are often referred to as profit-sharing agreements (PSAs).

Another potential energy bonanza lies in natural-gas production. While it is a less-developed industry in comparison to Azerbaijan's oil, its future appears to be similarly promising. Ninety-five percent of Azerbaijan's gas reserves lie beneath the Caspian.

Several offshore fields have been recently explored. One particular area, known as the Shah Deniz, is considered to be the world's largest natural gas find within the past quarter century. Discovered in 1999, it has already made Azerbaijan into a major gas exporter without any actual production. There is a great need for natural gas in nearby Turkey, which recently signed a 15-year agreement to have Azerbaijan become a major supplier in the future. Upon this contract's approval, Norway's Statoil and the Netherlands Royal Dutch Shell oil companies decided to jointly develop the Shah Deniz beginning in 2004.

Because of its location, Azerbaijan is emerging as a major transit center between Europe and Central Asia. Steady increases in shipping volume prompted the European Union to fund a program known as TRACEA (Transport System Europe-Caucasus-Asia) that will upgrade Baku's port facilities. The nation's railway and road systems also need major improvements: their infrastructure has considerably deteriorated since the Soviet era. In terms of air transport, Azerbaijan has regular service to nearly all of the former Soviet republics as well as several European countries, especially the United Kingdom, Germany, and the Netherlands. There are also many connections throughout the Middle East, from Iran to Israel.

Pipeline Politics

Pipeline networks are a critical part of Azerbaijan's economic picture. Baku is the processing point for Azerbaijan's energy yield, as well as for that of the Central Asian nations of Kazakhstan and Turkmenistan. These are energy-rich countries routing a significant amount of their production through Azerbaijan to reach European markets. Cargo ships currently handle this trade, and there are plans to increase Kazakhstan's and Turkmenistan's export capacities by building pipelines beneath the Caspian.

Russia has concerns about this proposal that cannot be ignored. Moscow objects to any Caspian venture in which it is not involved, in

In this 1998 photo, workers are preparing sections of the Western Route pipeline. The pipeline links Azerbaijan's Caspian Sea oil fields to a holding facility off the coast of the Georgian port of Supsa on the Black Sea. Because of limitations on the amount of oil that can be shipped through the route, a larger pipeline from Baku to Ceyhan, Turkey, has been constructed.

terms of both offshore extraction and routing. Azerbaijan recognized the likely problems Russia could cause if left out of the "contract of the century" agreement, so a Russian company was included in that project's consortium, mainly to allay its fears of a large Western presence in what had historically been czarist and Soviet domain. This has been standard practice in subsequent contracts, because offering Russia a stake in the development of the Caspian Sea lessens regional tensions.

Pipelines represent a similar dilemma. In order for Caspian oil to reach Western markets, shipments will have to be sent across land. Cost effectiveness is not the sole determinant. While sending the oil through existing networks would be the most economically feasible solution, politics and security are also influential factors. Many industry analysts believe that the best course for Caspian crude is via Iran's pipeline network to the Persian Gulf. This, however, will not happen. Although several American oil companies are involved in developing the Caspian, the United States government does not permit them to deal with the current regime in Iran, so the oil must be shipped another way.

The only operable networks lie in Russia and Georgia. While both are politically amicable toward the United States and other countries with a commercial presence in Azerbaijan, different problems exist.

The Russian pipeline is the larger of the two systems and can accommodate more oil flowing through its pipes. Linking Baku to the Black Sea port of Novorossiysk, it is commonly referred to as the Northern Route. However, the Northern Route is badly in need of repairs. The pipeline was built during the Soviet era, but its construction was of poor quality and prone to leakage. Maintenance is practically nonexistent. One estimate calculated that repairing the Northern Route would cost over $55 million.

There are other problems with shipping oil via the Northern Route. Novorossiysk can adequately handle offloading and storing up to 80 tons of Caspian oil per year. The port, however, is subject to frigid winter conditions and often has to suspend operations because of ice. Furthermore, the size of oil tankers sailing the Black Sea is limited, a consequence of the Turkish government's tightening ship regulations after several navigational mishaps in the Bosphorus Straits, the Black Sea's western outlet to the Mediterranean and beyond. Considering that the Bosphorus narrows to the size of a river when flowing past the city of Istanbul, and that approximately 1.5 million people cross between its European and Asian shores on an everyday basis, supertankers are not a good fit.

Yet another difficulty afflicts the Northern Route. A section of the pipeline runs through the politically unstable region of Chechnya, which is attempting to break away from Russia and form its own independent state. As a result, the Northern Route has often been sabotaged by Muslim extremists. This has forced Russia to build a new section of pipeline that bypasses Chechnya, although attacks sometimes still occur.

The second pipeline in Azerbaijan is known as the Western Route. It runs from Baku to Supsa, a port on the Black Sea in Georgia. Although this pipeline is shorter, Supsa is a small harbor that can only manage one-quarter the volume of petroleum that Novorossiysk processes. In addition, Supsa's Black Sea location subjects it to the same tanker restrictions with regard to shipping through the Bosphorus.

The Georgian pipeline system has its own security dilemmas as well. Part of the Western Route comes within ten miles of Nagorno-Karabakh. While Armenia currently occupies this disputed territory, it is the only Transcaucasian nation not involved with the current oil activity. Because Armenia has no stake in either the success of the Caspian's energy development or Azerbaijan's economic prospects, some experts fear that Armenia could try to subvert this enterprise. This has not yet happened, but, amid the continuing impasse over Nagorno-Karabakh, worries still remain.

Because of the shortcomings of the two existing pipelines, construction was started on a new pipeline. The new route will head southwards to the

Turkish port of Ceyhan via Georgia, and is scheduled to begin delivering oil by mid-2005. Building this Baku-Tbilisi-Ceyhan pipeline is more expensive than upgrading the existing infrastructure, but it has several advantages that make it worth its estimated $2.7 billion cost. Ceyhan is located on the Mediterranean Sea, and therefore solves the problem of vessel restrictions affecting Black Sea transport. It is also a larger, newer facility that is not subject to closing in winter.

The Baku-Tbilisi-Ceyhan route was a commercial decision, but it did not preclude politics. A percentage of Caspian oil will continue to flow along the Northern Route, primarily to preempt Russia's displeasure at its complete loss of control over transport or processing procedures. Also, the selection of the route itself was rooted in world politics. Ports in Armenia and Iran would be closer and more direct destinations for the pipeline

U.S. President Bill Clinton (center) speaks during a ceremony to mark the signing of the Baku-Tbilisi-Ceyhan pipeline agreement, November 1999. Clinton is flanked by Azerbaijan's president Haidar Aliyev (left) and Turkey's president Suleyman Demirel.

than Tbilisi, but Georgia has better relations with Azerbaijan and Western governments.

Other Economic Sectors

Azerbaijan's government recognizes that being totally dependent on the energy industry can hamper efforts to develop other economic sectors. In addition to oil and natural gas, Azerbaijan has other natural resources, such as iron ore, zinc, marble, and limestone. The Soviet period established a manufacturing base for chemical products, which is centered around Sumgayit, the nation's third-largest city. Much of the industrial sector is, however, in decrepit shape and needs substantial investment to modernize its facilities.

Agriculture employs the largest number of Azerbaijani workers. Forty percent of the nation's workforce is engaged in farming activities, primarily along the Kura and Araxes rivers. Cotton, grapes, and tobacco are the major cash crops. Agricultural production was severely affected by the political turmoil that followed the Soviet Union's collapse—one third of Azerbaijan's farming took place within Nagorno-Karabakh.

Under the Communist system, different parts of the Soviet Union were used to produce a single crop in order to maximize production. In Azerbaijan, cotton was usually cultivated at the expense of food crops; food was exported from other Soviet republics as needed. Between the end of World War II and the 1970s, Azerbaijan's cotton yield went from 500,000 to 5.5 million tons. However, the success of cotton farming has had a negative impact on Azerbaijan's environment. Chemical fertilizers, pesticides, and herbicides were used to boost production, leaving dangerously high toxic levels in the soil of many farm regions. This residue is often cited as the major cause of a noticeably high infant-mortality rate within Azerbaijan.

A herdsman guides sheep through the streets of his village in rural Azerbaijan. Agriculture employs two-fifths of all Azerbaijanis.

Governmental Administration

Azerbaijan's governmental infrastructure consists of 59 provinces known as *rayons*, 11 cities, and one autonomous republic (Nakhichevan). Its legal system is based on the concept of civil law; suffrage, or the right to vote, begins at 18 years of age. There is a separation of the executive, judicial, and legislative branches. That is similar to many Western governmental structures. The constitution was ratified in November 1995.

The national flag of Azerbaijan was designed during its first independence period (1918–20). It consists of three wide stripes of different colors. The upper half is blue and meant to represent Azerbaijan's Turkic origins. Its middle is red and stands for modernization and democracy. The green bottom symbolizes Azerbaijan's place within Islamic civilization. In the center of the red stripe is a white crescent, which also reflects Azerbaijan's

Islamic heritage, and an eight-pointed star that is said to acknowledge the nation's Zoroastrian origins. A more overt reference to Zoroastrianism is displayed in the national emblem, which was adopted in 1993 and shows the eight-pointed star surrounding a robust flame. This symbol is displayed on all Azerbaijani government buildings and diplomatic missions.

Executive Branch

Azerbaijan's president is the nation's most powerful official. The term of office lasts for five years with an opportunity to be reelected an extra term. Azerbaijan's latest presidential election was held in October 2003 and won by Ilham Aliyev, who received almost 77 percent of the vote.

One of the president's primary responsibilities is to supervise enactment of various laws and decrees. He also determines the nation's domestic and foreign policies. There are two administrative bodies within the

The flag of Azerbaijan, originally designed in 1918, was adopted when the country became independent in 1991.

executive branch that assist in the president's decision-making process: the Cabinet of Ministers and the Security Council.

The Cabinet of Ministers is the president's administrative authority. It consists of the prime minister, his deputies, and the directors of various governmental ministries. Unlike the president and the members of the legislative branch, the members of the Cabinet of Ministers are not elected officials who serve for constitutionally specified periods of time, although members of the Cabinet of Ministers must resign each time a new president takes office.

The prime minister is the cabinet's senior official and is appointed by the president in coordination with the legislature. The president can forgo legislative approval, however, if there is disagreement over his nomination for prime minister. Although a prime minister is immune from prosecution or even investigation during his term of office, the president determines the length of his service.

The Security Council was primarily established in response to the Nagorno-Karabakh crisis. Its mission is to protect Azerbaijan's independence and territorial integrity. The president determines the agenda at Security Council sessions, which, along with the prime minister and head of legislature, mainly comprise officials from what are referred to as "power" ministries—Defense, Internal Affairs, and National Security.

Legislative and Judicial Branches

The National Assembly, popularly known by its Azerbaijani term Milli Majlis, has 125 seats, with each member representing a particular electoral district. Its members are elected to serve five-year terms. The next legislative elections are scheduled to be held in November 2005. It will be the first time that all members are selected by popular vote. In past elections, 25 of the legislature's seats were determined by a system of indirect balloting known as proportional representation.

At present, the composition of the Milli Majlis is subject to intense debate and controversy. Based on the November 2000 election results, the assembly is overwhelmingly controlled by pro-Aliyev supporters. The New Azerbaijan Party, founded by Haidar Aliyev in 1995, and its allies hold 108 of the assembly's seats. The Popular Front is the largest opposition group, with 6 seats.

Due to this overwhelming discrepancy, there are questions as to whether the Milli Majlis truly represents the public will. The Popular Front and other opposition groups have refused to take their seats, charging electoral fraud and intimidation. They view the assembly as little more than a rubber-stamping session for the Aliyev family and its interests. Most Western observers who monitor Azerbaijan's elections agree with this perspective and advocate major legislative changes. Save for the change in voting procedures, the government favors political stability over comprehensive reforms.

A woman votes in Azerbaijan's October 2003 presidential election. Both men and women over age 18 are eligible to vote in national elections.

Azerbaijan's legal system includes a system of criminal, civil, and administrative courts that rule on cases in local jurisdictions. The Supreme Court is the country's highest court, and it decides cases brought to it on appeal from local courts. A Constitutional Court settles disputes between branches of Azerbaijan's government. Recently, individuals were allowed to submit cases to the

Constitutional Court. The president nominates Supreme and Constitutional Court judges, but they must be approved by the Milli Majlis.

Islam in Azerbaijan

Despite having a population that is over 90 percent Muslim, there is no official state religion in Azerbaijan. Article 18 of the Azerbaijani constitution allows for all faiths to practice their religion freely. Azerbaijan's major non-Muslim religions are Russian Orthodox and Armenian Orthodox Christianity, as well as Judaism. Combined, the followers of these faiths make up less than 7 percent of the total population.

About 75 percent of Azerbaijan's Muslim population follow Shia Islam; the remainder are Sunni Muslims. Shiite Islam is particularly predominant in southern Azerbaijan, especially along the border with Iran and Nakhichevan. Sunni Islam prevails throughout the northern part of the republic. A major reason for this regional difference lies in cultural orientation: the religious culture of southern Azerbaijan reflects its cross-border links with Shiite Iran, which go back to the Safavid period, while the north is populated by the Turkish-influenced Sunni.

Islam in Azerbaijan is administered by the Muslim Spiritual Board of the Transcaucasus, which is headquartered in Baku. Based on proportional numbers, the Spiritual Board's chairman is a Shiite, the deputy Sunni.

Islamic fervor is very limited in Azerbaijan. One study estimates that less than one-tenth of Azerbaijani Muslims consider themselves to be ardent believers. Relations between the Sunni and Shiite communities are comparatively better here than in much of the Islamic world. The absence of religious zeal, however, does not extend to the nation's cultural identity. Islam still has a certain influence on customs and traditions.

Azerbaijani views on Islam are best illustrated by the Shiite festival known as Ashura, which includes a passion play that involves frenzied wailing and even self-flagellation. The annual ceremony centers around the martyrdom of Hussein, the grandson of Muhammad and son of Ali, who was killed while attempting to become the **caliph**, or ruler of the Islamic world. After the death of Muhammad, there had always been a group of believers who thought the Prophet's descendants should be the religious and political leaders. Ali had become the fourth caliph in 656, but he was assassinated five years later. Shiites believed Ali's sons were the rightful caliphs, and Hussein challenged the Umayyad family, whom he considered to be usurpers, for control over Islam. Hussein and some of his outnumbered followers were massacred at the Battle of Karbala in 680.

Sunlight streams through the windows of a mosque where Azerbaijani Muslims perform their daily prayers. More than 90 percent of the people of Azerbaijan follow Islam.

Ashura is a heroic tragedy that attracts nearly all Muslims of Azerbaijan. Whereas the devout observe Ashura's religious connotations, those who see Islam primarily as a cultural force value the festival as folklore, heeding its message to persevere despite overwhelming odds.

From this perspective, Ashura symbolizes Azerbaijan's Soviet legacy. During the Soviet era, Communist authorities had made strenuous efforts to curtail the practice of Islam. The official philosophy of state atheism prevailed, and Muslims were forbidden to pray and engage in other forms of worship. Continuous anti-religious propaganda was common, and programs forcibly assimilated Azerbaijanis into becoming model Soviet citizens.

By the 1980s, Islam had been reduced to little more than a cultural vestige with an uncertain future. Before the Communist takeover in 1920, there had been some 2,000 mosques in Azerbaijan. By the time of *glasnost* and *perestroika*, that number had dwindled to 16. There were estimated to be fewer than 70 **mullahs**, or Muslim clerics, in Azerbaijan. Because of this shortage, Sunni and Shiite rites were sometimes performed by the same mullah—a rare occurrence indeed, considering that in other parts of the world Sunnis and Shiites had historically been at odds.

This situation began to change with the Islamic revolution that occurred during 1978–79 in Iran. The overthrow of an authoritarian, U.S.-supported government, and establishment of an Islamic theocracy that was hostile to both the U.S. and the Soviet Union, shocked the Muslims of Central Asia. And as the Soviet Union began its reform programs of the 1980s, there came an Islamic revival. *Glasnost* permitted Azerbaijanis to celebrate previously forbidden festivals, such as Ashura, and to reopen and restore badly neglected mosques. As Communism headed toward collapse, Iran's Shiite clerics moved throughout Azerbaijan, spreading their fundamentalist gospel. Turkey opposed the growing Iranian influence with its own model of Islamic secularism, but the Sunni doctrine had limited appeal.

Iran's religious emissaries tend to exploit Islam for political purposes. The Islamic Party of Azerbaijan is a telling example. Established with Iranian support in the early 1990s, it advocated that newly independent Azerbaijan follow their benefactor's model and become an Islamic republic. Azerbaijani authorities suspected that the Islamic Party was spying for the Iranians and outlawed it.

The Islamic Party affair focused concern on missionary activities within Azerbaijan. Foreign proselytizers must register with the Muslim Spiritual Board for permission to visit local communities, but few bother doing so. Recent laws limit the number of pastors visiting Azerbaijan, and the length of their stay. While the primary function of these statutes is to better monitor Iran's Islamic endeavors, various Christian and other sects are also being watched.

Other Religions

There once was a sizeable non-Muslim presence within Azerbaijan, but when the nation became independent in 1991, uncertainty about the future led to mass exodus. The Russian (and, to a lesser extent, Armenian) outflow actually began during the post–World War II period, when Azerbaijan's oil production sharply declined. As Siberia became the Soviet Union's new energy center in the 1950s, many Russian professionals moved where they were needed in other parts of the Soviet Union. Although Armenians were also very involved in the oil industry, most stayed because of their cultural and historic ties to the Transcaucasus. This changed with the U.S.S.R.'s collapse and ensuing Nagorno-Karabakh crisis, and a predominantly Armenian wave of immigration followed in the early 1990s.

The Jewish presence in Azerbaijan dates back to pre-Islamic times. Most of the 16,000-strong community lives in Baku. Azerbaijan's Jews are either Ashkenazim (Jews of European descent who mainly came to

An elderly Jewish man waits to speak with the rabbi at the Vaad Lhotzola Hebrew School in downtown Baku. Because of the country's tolerance for all religions, the Jewish community in Azerbaijan has flourished for centuries.

Azerbaijan during the 19th-century oil boom), or a group known as Mountain Jews, who can trace their Transcaucasian background to the fifth century B.C. There is also a smaller presence of Georgian Jews, another congregation with a long regional history.

Throughout the centuries, Jews and Muslims have maintained very good relations in Azerbaijan. There are three synagogues in Baku, one each for the Mountain, Georgian, and Ashkenazim Jews. All share a

Community Cultural Center and Hebrew School for 300 students. Azerbaijan is also one of the few Muslim nations to have full diplomatic relations with Israel.

Approximately 40,000 Jews left Azerbaijan after the fall of the U.S.S.R. Most of them left for Israel, worried by economic uncertainty and the escalating tensions with Armenia. Many émigrés frequently return, however, either for business or family reasons.

An Azeri woman shows off a display of flatbreads in a shop in Baku. The Azeri are the largest ethnic group in Azerbaijan, making up about 90 percent of the population. Other groups include Dagestani and Russians. Most of Azerbaijan's small Armenian minority lives in the disputed Nagorno-Karabakh enclave.

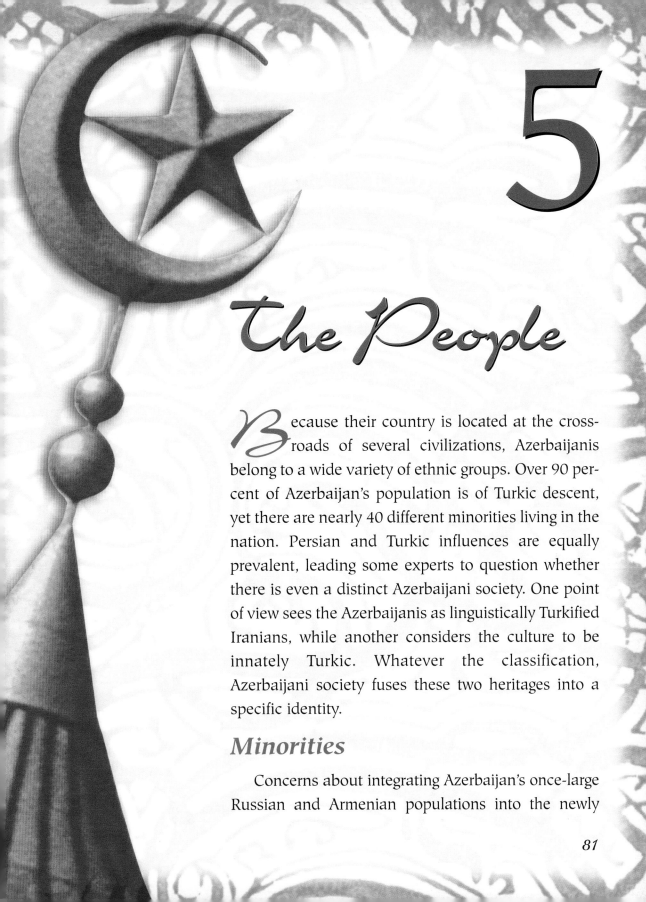

5

The People

Because their country is located at the cross-roads of several civilizations, Azerbaijanis belong to a wide variety of ethnic groups. Over 90 percent of Azerbaijan's population is of Turkic descent, yet there are nearly 40 different minorities living in the nation. Persian and Turkic influences are equally prevalent, leading some experts to question whether there is even a distinct Azerbaijani society. One point of view sees the Azerbaijanis as linguistically Turkified Iranians, while another considers the culture to be innately Turkic. Whatever the classification, Azerbaijani society fuses these two heritages into a specific identity.

Minorities

Concerns about integrating Azerbaijan's once-large Russian and Armenian populations into the newly independent environment have largely faded. Although both communities are still the nation's largest minorities, their political and economic dominance has dwindled as many Russians and Armenians have left Azerbaijan. Those who remain are mostly elderly or very poor, and they don't have either the wherewithal or the inclination to leave.

Geography poses the biggest challenge to establishing a common national character. Due to the mountainous isolation of regions within Azerbaijan, people consider their particular clan to be the primary source of allegiance, which periodically causes separatist problems for Azerbaijan. Despite centuries of foreign rule, this attitude never completely vanished. Several ethnic groups—the largest among them the Lezghin and the Talysh—are especially tight-knit.

The Lezghins are non-Turkic Sunni Muslims who live in northeastern Azerbaijan. This is the Greater Caucasus area, replete with hard-to-access canyons and gorges. Approximately 160,000 Lezghins live on the Azerbaijani side of this range, with a slightly larger group residing in an adjacent region of Russia known as Daghestan (in Turkic, "the land of many mountains"). The Lezghins claim to be descended from the historic kingdom of Albania. They have called for the creation of a "Lezghinistan" that would unite their Azerbaijani and Russian communities, and some periodically resort to terrorism in order to achieve this aim. While their movement has very limited support, it is nonetheless a barrier to forging national unity.

Along Azerbaijan's southeast border with Iran live an estimated 130,000 Talysh. They are Shiite Muslims who speak a language related to Persian, called Talyshi. The Talysh demands are less strident than the Lezghins' claims, yet during the early period of Azerbaijan's independence, they also wanted to have their own, autonomous region. Although this activity ceased when Haidar Aliyev came to power, a Talysh political party still exists.

Displaced Persons

Another vital matter confronting Azerbaijan's attempt to forge a national consensus concerns the thousands of people displaced by the conflict with Armenia. Some 850,000 Azerbaijani refugees—or one out of every nine residents of the nation—either fled from the Nagorno-Karabakh conflict or were forced out by Armenia. Over two-thirds of this population lives in temporary accommodations, ranging from public buildings to tent camps and even abandoned railway cars.

While Azerbaijanis sympathize with their brethren's plight, tensions do arise. The influx has badly strained the country's health and educational systems, as well as employment services. For a nation in which nearly half of the population lives in poverty, the war refugees have become an unwel-

Since 1992, Azeri refugee families from Nagorno-Karabakh have lived in old railroad boxcars in this camp near the town of Saatli, Azerbaijan, hoping for an opportunity to return to their homes.

The People of Azerbaijan

Population: 7,868,385

Ethnic Groups: Azerbaijani 90%; Dagestani (Lezghin and other minorities residing in the Greater Caucasus region) 3.2%; Russian 2.5%; Armenian 2% (almost al in the Nagorno-Karabakh region); other 2.3% (1998 est.)

Age Structure:
    0–14 years: 27%
    15–64 years: 65%
    65 years and over: 8%

Population Growth Rate: 0.52%

Birth Rate: 19.81 births/1,000 population

Death Rate: 9.76 deaths/1,000 population

Life Expectancy at Birth:
    Total population: 63.25 years
    Males: 59.09 years
    Females: 67.62 years

Total Fertility Rate: 2.39 children born/woman

Religions: Muslim 93.4%: Russian Orthodox 2.5%; Armenian Orthodox 2.3%; others 1.8% (1995 est.)

Languages: Azeri, Russian, Armenian. Very small minorities speak other languages

Literacy: 97% (1989)

All figures are 2004 estimates unless otherwise noted.
Source: Adapted from CIA World Factbook, 2004.

come burden. It is worth noting that the displaced Azerbaijanis have not yet channeled their frustration into a political movement. Studies show that they are too busy scrambling to make ends meet to organize and collectively voice their concerns. Their continued presence, however, constantly reminds the nation that all attempts to achieve a harmonious and stable atmosphere will continue to fail until the refugees' plight is resolved.

Language and Script

Azerbaijan's language, known as Azeri, originated in Central Asia between A.D. 600 and 1000. It closely resembles the language that is spoken today in Turkey and the Central Asian nation of Turkmenistan. All these nations are part of a linguistic division known as Turkic.

Iran has the largest number of Azeri speakers. It is that nation's second language after Persian, which is also called Farsi. The reason so many—between 13 and 16 million—Iranian citizens are conversant in Azeri is the 19th-century border partitions between Russia and Persia, which split the Azerbaijani population.

During the last 80 years, the Azeri script has undergone several changes. Before the Soviet takeover, it was customary to write in Arabic; this practice had lasted for over 1,200 years. The Arabic alphabet, however, was not the best choice for transliterating the vocal sounds of Azeri. Educational reformers argued that Latin lettering was better suited to Turkic languages, believing it would end the high rates of illiteracy throughout Azerbaijan and Central Asia. Traditionalists thought otherwise, defending Arabic as the continuation of Islamic heritage amid Russian rule. The controversy was ultimately settled by Communist authorities, who decreed in 1924 that Azeri officially use the Latin script.

Azerbaijan was the first of the Soviet Muslim republics to Latinize its alphabet. The change began to show positive results fighting illiteracy, which aroused interest from nearby Turkey. The Turks were eager to sever their Ottoman past and become a modern nation oriented toward the West. Following Azerbaijan's example, in 1928 Turkey also adopted Latin lettering.

Turkey's decision worried Soviet officials. One of the reasons why Moscow supported Latinization was the idea that Azerbaijan would become isolated from its Islamic culture, which would reduce the threat of anti-Communist insurgency. While Turkey wasn't a Muslim republic, its

A man reads a newspaper in which some articles are typeset using the Cyrillic alphabet while others are printed using the Latin alphabet, July 31, 2001. The next day, according to government decree, all newspapers and other publications in Azerbaijan were to use only the Latin alphabet.

nationalist philosophy could readily influence Azerbaijan if they used the same written language.

In order to prevent this from happening, the Azeri alphabet was altered yet again. This time, Cyrillic, the script used in the Russian language, became Azerbaijan's official lettering in 1940. The change, aimed to create a loyal Soviet citizenry, further separated Azerbaijanis from their cultural bearings. This was Communism's notorious Stalinist period, and the rulers of the Soviet Union did not care whether Cyrillic was suitable for transliteration of Azeri words.

Azerbaijan's Cyrillic era lasted over 50 years, until the U.S.S.R. disintegrated. The alphabet issue arose once again for newly independent

Azerbaijan, focusing on whether the nation should return to Latin or Arabic script. After serious debate, it was decided not to bring back the latter, with all its linguistic shortcomings. For the fourth time in less than 70 years, Azerbaijan adopted a new script, revising the 1920s Latin version of Azeri to meet computer-age requirements.

While Azerbaijan planned to change from Cyrillic to Latin by 1993, political instability suspended the process. For nearly a decade, the nation was a hodgepodge of different letterings. Arabic newsprint competed with Cyrillic street signs and Latin advertisements. The result was a disjointed state of affairs throughout the nation. In the summer of 2001, Haidar Aliyev issued a decree banning further usage of any script other than Latin.

While there are now stiff penalties for the usage of Cyrillic, old habits endure. Many Azerbaijanis who were educated in Cyrillic prefer to keep using it as their primary form of communication. This is especially the case with Azerbaijan's elderly, who feel alienated from the Latin-oriented society. This group has little interest in adapting to the new requirements, so Azerbaijan will unofficially remain a bilingual community for the foreseeable future.

The Family

The typical Azerbaijani family is struggling. While the post-Soviet environment promises future affluence, mostly due to the nation's energy resources, few people have actually benefited from these ventures so far. Corruption is a factor, but for the most part current circumstances can be explained by the nation's transforming itself into a capitalist society. In Soviet times, Azerbaijan's governmental bureaucracies determined the nation's economic goals and standards. Independence ended this procedure, and commercial targets are no longer assigned by the government but decided upon by a free market. The change in commercial systems has traumatized those used to Communism's guidance and procedures, yet most younger Azerbaijanis have quickly adapted.

Despite experiencing over a century of modernization that began with the great oil boom, Azerbaijani families are still steeped in tradition. A typical household is headed by the male elder, who is clearly the decision maker. Elder women can also be very influential in certain matters, especially marriage.

Clan or provincial loyalties still tend to take precedence when it comes to relationships. Soviet-era apartment complexes are often populated by residents who come predominantly from the same region. Choices in friendships and even arranged marriages can also generally be traced to this mentality.

A woman's life in Azerbaijan is less restricted when compared to other Islamic societies. The Soviet era ended the wearing of veils and long robes that had defined feminine clothing here for centuries. Communism, in fact, liberated Azerbaijani women from a narrow existence between the household and the marketplace. They attended school without any religious or cultural restraints, and were encouraged to enter the workforce. Many became important professionals and government officials, a development that would have been impossible during czarist times.

Despite these advancements, certain limitations remain. Nearly all unmarried Azerbaijani women live with their parents, obeying strict curfews. Dating has its own particular codes, from which Azerbaijani males are exempt. Going out with foreigners or someone unknown to the family is frowned upon. Public displays of affection are not seen in a positive light. Those who have a higher degree of independence can act with greater liberty but risk being ostracized.

In the countryside, women are even more restricted. Not only are marriages arranged for them by their families, but the custom of paying a "bride price" still exists. The inability to carry out this ritual can cause

Unlike some other predominantly Muslim countries, women in Azerbaijan do not have to veil themselves when they go out in public. Many women are educated and serve in professional or government positions.

ridicule for a groom and his family. In order to avoid financial embarrassment, poor young men have kidnapped their prospective matches rather than adhere to tradition.

Food

Azerbaijani cuisine is a combination of Georgian, Turkish, Iranian, and Central Asian influences. While it has much in common with its neighbors' styles of cooking, Azerbaijan has its own traditional dishes and preparation methods. There is a heavy emphasis on richly spiced meats, especially lamb, beef, and poultry.

Among Azerbaijanis' favorite dishes are pilaf (also known as *plov*), which is fried rice that's usually mixed with meat, fish, vegetables, and

Azerbaijan boasts some of the world's best caviar. There are three classifications for quality. Beluga is the highest grade and the most expensive; most of its production is exported. Osetra and Sevruga are lesser grade but more affordable. No matter the quality, or the fact that it is fish eggs, caviar is worth tasting.

even fruit. Eggplants, spinach, beets, and cabbage are also part of the standard fare. Many dishes use saffron, mint, parsley, and aniseed for spicing.

One of the nation's basic staples is *kebab,* a selection of small pieces of meat or vegetables threaded onto a thin wooden skewer and grilled. *Bosartma* is an Azerbaijani favorite, served with vegetables and plum sauce, or, in warmer weather, with lemon slices and cucumbers. Another common dish is *dolma*—grape leaves usually stuffed with minced lamb, tomatoes, peppers, and onions. Chestnuts, peas, rice, and even apples are sometimes part of the mix. Yogurt is often used as the sauce, adding extra flavor to *dolma.*

There are also regional cuisines. In northeast Azerbaijan, *khangal,* whose ingredients include meat, fried onions, and dried cottage cheese, is popular. Going toward the Iranian border, one can find stuffed chickens and fish baked in tandoori ovens. Around Baku, there is *dushpara*—small dumplings that consist of meat stuffing wrapped in a piece of very thin dough.

Most of these dishes involve lengthy preparation, however, and are better suited for family gatherings or holidays. Due to budget limitations, an Azerbaijani's daily fare is relatively simpler. Soups are a mainstay during the winter; they are usually made from condensed yogurt, mixed with meatballs, peas, and herbs. Pilaf is frequently served, as are breads, the most common being round loaves called *chorek*, and *lavash*, a thick, soft local version of pita bread.

Breakfast is a rather mundane affair, save for a culinary adventure known as *hash* (pronounced as "khash"). This is usually the boiled hoof of a lamb or cow, served with vinegar. The end product is a gelatinous broth that is salvaged with shots of vodka. It is a hearty concoction for cold winter mornings, but not recommended as a dietary staple.

Vodka consumption is not only a hangover from years of Russian rule, but also reflects Azerbaijan's flexible attitude toward Islamic edicts. Islam forbids alcohol, and it is banned in neighboring Iran. Azerbaijan, however, has had longer exposure to Western customs than most Muslim societies—

Fresh fruit is sold at these stalls on the streets of Baku.

nearly 200 years of Russian presence was bound to sway cultural attitudes. It should also be noted that while Azerbaijanis tolerate alcohol, the nation, unlike other former Soviet republics, does not have a drinking problem.

Tea (called *chai*) is Azerbaijan's most common drink. It is drunk in small glasses, and can be served with various jams, nuts, and dried fruit. In a nod to Russian influence, tea is sometimes mixed with jam and served at the end of a meal. There's also homage to Persian and Turkic cultures in the form of teahouses, which are essentially social clubs for men to get together over cigarettes and chai.

Caviar is Azerbaijan's edible "black gold." It is rows of fish eggs produced by a particular fish, the sturgeon. Caspian Sea caviar is one of the world's most coveted gourmet items, and is therefore a very expensive product. It is common fare for the Azerbaijani diet, however, readily served with other foods or just as a meal by itself. Unfortunately, the sturgeon population has severely dwindled due to years of overfishing. The situation has become so critical that a ban on exporting caviar was recently enacted to help rebuild stock. There are attempts to stop poaching—or illegal fishing—but it is a very difficult task, considering demand for caviar despite its exorbitant prices.

Education

A reflection of the emphasis that Azerbaijanis place upon education is the number of teachers employed in the nation. Forty-four percent of Azerbaijan's government workers are educators, the second-largest employment sector after agriculture. They instruct 1.63 million students, or more than one-fifth of the republic's population.

Despite its multiple deficiencies, Soviet rule did establish an impressive educational system. Prior to it, Azerbaijan's literacy rate hovered around 10 percent, and most of these Azerbaijani children's educational experiences were limited to religious training. A tiny number of women were allowed to attend school. There were some improvements during the czarist era, but these mainly benefited ethnic Russians and other European minorities.

The Soviet regime believed in education for all, regardless of sex or ethnic background. Besides switching Azeri to the more accessible Latin alphabet, Soviet authorities mandated that all youngsters attend school for an eight-year period. By the late 1950s, Azerbaijan's literacy rate reached 97 percent.

Due to the role of oil in Azerbaijan's economy, several technical institutes were established, which ensured that a relatively high number of Azerbaijanis have received degrees in scientific and industrial fields. These facilities attracted people from all over the Soviet Union, and, although they are presently strapped for funding, continue to do so, noticeably drawing students from Central Asia. Among the most prestigious establishments are Azerbaijan's Academy of Sciences, the Polytechnic Institute, and the Institute of Petroleum and Chemical Industry.

Azerbaijan's post-Communist environment has altered certain programs. Religion is now taught, whereas during the Soviet period it had been banned. Enrollment in classes teaching the Russian language have been steadily declining, and mandatory courses in Communist ideology have been eliminated altogether. Western-style education has become a popular concept. Within the past decade, in Baku, two universities have been established, which use English as the primary language for instruction.

The Arts and Literature

Azerbaijan has given the Islamic world some of its finest poetry. It mixes Iranian and Turkic traditions and is usually based on stories that predate Islam. The most prominent Azerbaijani poets are Nizami Gangevi, who lived during the 10th and early 11th centuries, and Mohammed ibn

Suleiman Fizuli (1492–1556). Fizuli was a resident of Baghdad, yet he wrote in Azeri. Using the pen name Khatai, Shah Ismail I, who founded Persia's Safavid Dynasty in 1501, displayed his cultural roots by composing Azeri verses.

Nizami (as he is popularly known), is particularly revered in Azerbaijan. His most famous work is a collection of five epic poems known as the *Khamseh*. One of these odes, *Layla and Majnun*, has been compared to *Romeo and Juliet* in its lyrical beauty.

A significant part of the literary heritage revolves around folklore. This is represented by epic stories known as *dastans*, which reflect Turkic traditions. Usually recited to music, *dastans* deal with such themes as heroism, morality, and tribal customs. *The Book of Dede Korkut* and *Koroghlu* are the best-known narratives that use *dastan* techniques.

Modern Azerbaijani literature is less acclaimed. While during the Soviet period the reading audience had grown, writers were particularly targeted during the Great Terror. They were either exiled or executed, which wiped out a whole generation of literary talent. *Glasnost* began a new period, stimulating an intellectual revival that created several literary magazines and encouraged new authors.

Azerbaijani theater is noticeably influenced by European theatrical traditions. In the 19th century, Azerbaijan earned a reputation within the Islamic world for pioneering new ideas in satire and drama. The nation's leading playwright was Mirza Fath Ali Akhundzade, who saw theater as the perfect medium for spreading ideas to a largely illiterate public. Inspired by Europe's 18th-century Enlightenment period, he wrote about the social ills of contemporary society.

Theater was nationalized in Soviet times. Authorities closely supervised repertories and censored the plays they performed. Theaters were strongly encouraged to stage plays that glorified the Communist way of life. On the other hand, the performing arts benefited from state control.

Nizami Gangevi (right) was one of the greatest Persian-language poets; his face graces Azerbaijan's currency and nearly every town has a street named after him. The National Museum of Azerbaijan Literature (above) was originally dedicated solely to Nizami's legacy.

Opera and ballet were given steady financial backing, a nagging problem in today's unhindered yet irregular environment.

Entertainment

Compared to a decade ago, there are more entertainment choices in Azerbaijan. During Soviet times, organized amusement was mandatory. The outlets were limited, usually to state-produced cinema and musical concerts. Television, newspapers, and even museums were one-dimensional reflections of Communist propaganda and philosophy. Travel was essentially restricted to local outings.

As shown by today's media, this stifling atmosphere has changed. Azerbaijani television now has several independent, and even internation-

Azerbaijani musicians play traditional music.

al (Turkish and Russian), transmissions. Over 50 newspapers and magazines are available, nearly all of them published in Baku, among them many independent ones competing with government- and party-financed periodicals. *Ayma-Zerkalo* ("Mirror") is a highly popular weekly newspaper, entirely supported by its advertising sales rather than institutional backing. The film industry is another matter. A once-vibrant operation, it has practically ceased due to scarce investment.

The music scene has fared better. Azerbaijanis regularly attend concerts ranging from classical to jazz. The nation has a long tradition of composers and performers, the most famous being Mstislav Rostropovich, the world's most esteemed cellist.

Boxing and wrestling have traditionally been Azerbaijan's most popular sports. The nation has already established an international reputation in freestyle wrestling, winning medals at the Olympics and other tournaments. Soccer is also very popular, with several clubs competing at local and national levels.

Holidays and Popular Celebrations

Novruz is Azerbaijan's favorite holiday. It has been celebrated for 3,000 years and celebrates the spring equinox on March 21. As implied by its timing, Novruz (which means "new day") is a time of renewal and rebirth. The festival's origins are believed to be rooted in the Zoroastrian religion. Despite its non-Islamic character and Soviet attempts to suppress Novruz, the holiday is an integral part of Azerbaijani culture. It is also celebrated throughout Turkic and Persian societies.

A major theme in Novruz is cleanliness. Several days prior to festivities, families busy themselves with washing, waxing, and even repainting their homes. Children and the elderly are usually given new clothes as presents.

The lighting of bonfires is another noted aspect. Angels supposedly recognize these blazes as a signal to visit the earth. Dressed as spirits, children jump over the flames, and bang kitchenware, wishing their neighbors good fortune and asking for treats.

The Muslim holy month of Ramadan is also observed. Because Ramadan is based on the Islamic calendar, which uses the moon's cycles as its time standard, the event occurs at a different time each year. Those who religiously follow this period must fast during the daytime. The intention is to identify with those unable to afford food or other basic comforts. When the sun goes down, practitioners resume eating, storing their energy for another day of abstinence. The final day of Ramadan is Eid al-Fitr ("breaking of the fast"), which is celebrated with large feasts and congratulatory parties.

Along with cultural and religious holidays, there are also secular ones. The most prominent observances are related to Azerbaijan's political history. There are actually two independence days, celebrating the proclamation of the nation's first state in 1918 (Republic Day), and secession from the U.S.S.R. in 1991 (National Independence Day). A more solemn ceremony is Martyrs' Day on January 20, commemorating those who lost their lives during the 1990 Black January crisis.

This view of Baku shows the Muhammad mosque and busy harbor. Baku is by far the largest city in Azerbaijan, home to about two-fifths of the country's population.

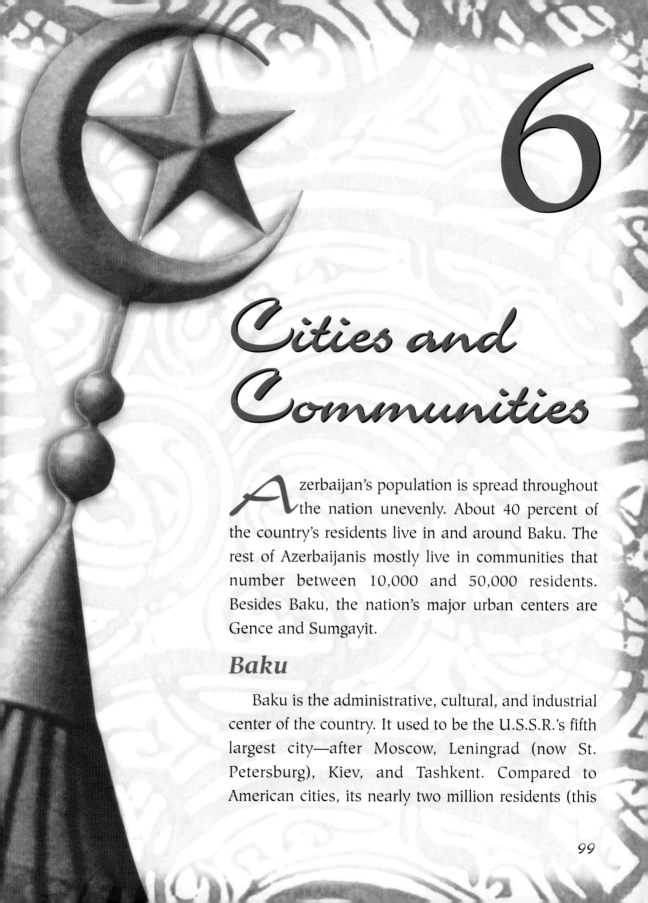

6

Cities and Communities

zerbaijan's population is spread throughout the nation unevenly. About 40 percent of the country's residents live in and around Baku. The rest of Azerbaijanis mostly live in communities that number between 10,000 and 50,000 residents. Besides Baku, the nation's major urban centers are Gence and Sumgayit.

Baku

Baku is the administrative, cultural, and industrial center of the country. It used to be the U.S.S.R.'s fifth largest city—after Moscow, Leningrad (now St. Petersburg), Kiev, and Tashkent. Compared to American cities, its nearly two million residents (this

The lights of Baku at night.

is a rough estimate that does not take into account the refugee influx from Nagorno-Karabakh) make it about the size of Houston, Texas. There are essentially three cities within Baku—the historic Old Town or "Inner City," rimmed by the 19th-century oil-boom neighborhoods, and the Soviet-built areas that surround those.

Icheri Sehir ("Inner City") is an intriguing maze of narrow alleys and winding passages dating back to the pre-Russian period. It is surrounded by high fortress walls that nearly extend down to a section of Baku's Caspian shoreline. On the edge of *Icheri Sehir* stands Baku's best-known landmark, the 11th-century Maiden's Tower. Legends abound about the way this structure got its name, but one thing is known for a fact: it is the city's oldest building, with a sweeping view of Baku's harbor from the top. In the center of *Icheri Sehir* is the Shervan Shah Palace, which was built in the 15th and 16th century by the Khanate of Baku. The palace is actually a compound with a royal chamber, mosque, and mausoleum. It accurately reflects what an Azerbaijani principality looked like until such principalities were abolished by Persian and Russian conquerors. In recent years, *Icheri Sehir*'s ancient streets have become Baku's trendiest and most expensive neighborhood, due to foreign companies taking up residence there.

Within walking distance of *Icheri Sehir* is a Soviet-era complex known as Fountain Square. Surrounding this area are several streets with stately buildings, dating back to the late 19th and early 20th centuries. Many of these structures are mansions built during Baku's oil-boom days, which give the city a uniquely European feel. Some have even been turned into museums reflecting the opulence that once existed before Communism.

The Fountain Square area, with its many shops and restaurants, is also Baku's commercial hub. Going in the direction of the Caspian, its streets lead to a seaside park, with shady paths that are ideal for picnics and leisurely strolls. Dominating the horizon is an imitation oil derrick that shows the time and temperature. In general, Baku is a safe place to walk around, but, as in any big city, it has areas that should be avoided, especially after dark.

Spreading out from *Icheri Sehir* and Fountain Square are districts built during Soviet times. They are, essentially, nondescript housing projects where Baku's workforce lives. Most people who live here are either employed in the energy industry or work for the government. There are also a fair number of small **entrepreneurs** within these neighborhoods, satisfying growing local demands for goods and services. Many operations are conveniently located stalls that sell refreshments, produce, and merchandise that would otherwise have to be purchased miles away in the city's center.

Transportation is another popular outlet for urban self-employment. Baku has buses, trolleys, and even a subway system, but they are very unreliable when it comes to service. While there are licensed taxis, most Bakintsy (residents of Baku), if pressed for time, will flag down private cars and negotiate a ride. Hiring private drivers is another alternative, yet few wage-earners can afford it. Sharing taxis is the preferred way of getting around in Baku, as well as the rest of Azerbaijan. Shuttle buses are plentiful, go to areas that Baku's mass transit does not reach, and are reasonably priced.

In one of the more affluent Soviet-built neighborhoods overlooking the Caspian Sea lies the Martyrs' Cemetery. Formerly a park, it became a burial ground honoring the Azerbaijanis who lost their lives during Black January and the Nagorno-Karabakh conflict. On the headstone of each grave is a photograph of the person underneath, most of whom were very young.

Gence

With a population of 278,000, Gence (pronounced "ganja") is Azerbaijan's second-largest city. It is located 186 miles (300 km) west of Baku, on the northeastern edge of the Lower Caucasus range. Surrounded by several lakes and lush mountain scenery, Gence is considered one of Azerbaijan's prettiest towns. The major industries are textiles and carpet manufacturing.

Founded in the fifth century, Gence has a longer, more varied history than Baku. For many centuries—from the Albanian period through Seljuk, Mongol, and Safavid reigns—it was Azerbaijan's cultural and commercial center. Russia's Czar Alexander I annexed the city from Persia in 1804, renaming it Elizavetopol, after his wife. This name would last for over a century, until the Russian Revolution overthrew czarist rule.

Gence played a prominent role in Azerbaijan's 1918–20 independence period and its immediate aftermath. It was the first capital of the Azerbaijan Democratic Republic, but eventually that honor became Baku's. Gence is also remembered in Azerbaijani national lore as the city that staged a major rebellion against the newly established Soviet regime in 1920. This was a bloody revolt, which inevitably resulted in hundreds of executions and mass exiles of Azerbaijani rebels.

Communist authorities were eager to eradicate any symbols of Azerbaijani nationalism, and so they renamed Gence yet again in the 1930s. It became known as Kirovabad, in honor of a Soviet official who

Most Azerbaijanis live in small villages nestled in the mountains. One of these is Lahic, which is known for its traditional crafts, particularly in copperware.

had recently died. This name lasted for nearly six decades, until the Soviet Union's collapse, whereupon Gence's real name was formally restored one more time.

There are several structures that reflect the city's long history. Among the most notable are the 17th-century Shah Abbas Mosque and Gence's former city hall, where Azerbaijan's earliest public meetings took place. There is an airport, and a frequent bus service connects Gence to Baku.

Sumgayit

This grim industrial city of 275,000 people lies 25 miles (40 km) west of Baku on the Apsheron Peninsula. Once a sleepy fishing village, it became a major manufacturing site as well as Azerbaijan's third-largest city during World War II. Baku's nearby petroleum fields provide the raw material for Sumgayit's output, including such byproducts as synthetic rubber and chemical fertilizers.

Unfortunately, Sumgayit is considered to be one of the world's most polluted places. If there is any reason to visit Sumgayit, it is to see the

> In contrast with its current atmosphere, Sumgayit's name is said to derive from a romantic legend. The city is located on a river that, centuries ago, had its approach to the Caspian Sea blocked by a monster. The community asked one of its citizens, a warrior named Sum, to slay the creature, which he successfully did. However, when the river started flowing again, Sum was swept away. Jeyran, Sum's beloved, refused to believe he had died and would go to the river's edge for the rest of her life, shouting *"Sum, gayit!"* ("Sum, return!").

environmental damage that rapid industrialization can cause. The Soviet buildup proceeded without any safeguards, exacting a terrible toll on this city's population. Sumgayit once had the Soviet Union's highest infant mortality rate. Its population still suffers from a wide array of physical and psychological ailments.

Adding insult to injury, Sumgayit's infrastructure is now too obsolete to compete in today's world economy. The city needs a large amount of foreign investment to modernize its industrial facilities, or it will turn into a virtual ghost town. In order to attract business, Sumgayit recently became a free economic zone, which allows foreign companies to establish themselves without having to pay taxes or to comply with a burdensome amount of governmental regulations.

Other Places of Interest

Quba (also known as Guba or Kuba) is a picturesque town in the Greater Caucasus region. It is located in an agricultural area that is renowned for its apple orchards, which, come springtime, cover Quba with blossoms. The town of 22,000 is also a carpet-making center, considered one of the finest within the Caucasus region.

Quba boasts a lot of well-preserved buildings. Among the more notable are a 16th-century fortress and a unique, octagonally shaped mosque. An ancient Zoroastrian temple stands not far from the city.

Adjacent to Quba is the town of Krasnaya Sloboda, which is known for being a center of Mountain Jewish culture since the 13th century. It used to be known as Yevreyskaya Sloboda ("Jewish settlement"), until the Communists came to power. Not only did they change the name to Krasnaya Sloboda ("Red Settlement"), they also severely restricted the town's religious nature. Eleven synagogues existed in Krasnaya Sloboda before the Great Terror began; only one still stood by the beginning of World War II.

However, the Mountain Jewish community survived. Most local residents have now emigrated to Israel, yet they have not forgotten their roots. They send money to their relatives in Krasnaya Sloboda, which allows for the preservation and reconstruction of several synagogues.

North, toward the country of Georgia, lies the historic community of Sheki (also called Saki, Shaki, Nukha, or Nuha), which gets its name from a local tribe. Its origins go back to the Bronze Age, and throughout history the Albanian, Arab, Mongol, and Safavid dynasties have occupied the community. Sheki also used to be a flourishing khanate known for its silk production. Soviet rule recognized Sheki's economic renown, and the largest silk plant within the U.S.S.R. was built there. The factory still exists, but now it operates at a fraction of its former capacity.

An 18th-century palace aptly represents Sheki's past. It is a two-story structure that houses magnificent frescos and stained-glass work. A fortress surrounds the building, and there is a museum of silk artifacts on its grounds. Another symbol of Sheki's commercial past is its ***caravanserai***, one of the ancient inns built along the legendary Silk Road to accommodate merchants traveling between Europe and Asia. Sheki's *caravanserai* had been discarded for centuries as a useless relic of the past, but was recently renovated to become the town's main hotel.

Azerbaijani president Ilham Aliyev meets with his Russian counterpart Vladimir Putin prior to a meeting of the Commonwealth of Independent States (CIS) in Yalta. Russia continues to exert considerable influence over Azerbaijan's regional policies.

7

Foreign Relations

Azerbaijan today faces several important foreign policy challenges. Besides the nation's burgeoning oil wealth and its strategically important location on the world stage, Azerbaijan must carefully balance the interests of Russia, Iran, and the West. Haidar Aliyev maintained a successful equilibrium between these forces, enabling Azerbaijan to stay its own independent course. It is still too soon to discern whether the country will stay on its previous path or head in another direction under Ilham Aliyev, who became president in late 2003. Because he lacks his father's experience and even an unquestioned hold on power, there are concerns that Ilham will not successfully adapt to statesmanship. For the time being, he keeps his options open, evaluating Russian, Iranian, and Western positions.

There are indications, however, that a clearly defined doctrine is taking shape. One of President Aliyev's senior advisors recently wrote that despite its Islamic ties to Asia, Azerbaijan made a strategic commitment to become a European state after regaining independence 13 years ago.

The major components characterizing Azerbaijani foreign policy are: (1) regionalism, which centers on working with other Caspian states in developing energy resources; (2) "Atlanticism"—cooperating with the United States in combating terrorism; and, most important, (3) "Eurocentrism"—participating in European security structures, particularly the North Atlantic Treaty Organization (NATO). These three categories incorporate the various economic, strategic, and cultural aspects of Azerbaijan's foreign policy.

Regionalism

Azerbaijan's regional policy primarily revolves around its relations with Russia and Iran. Other nations involved in energy production and transport—principally Kazakhstan, Turkmenistan, and Georgia—are part of this category.

Although Russia no longer controls Azerbaijan, as the major regional power it still plays an important role. There are too many cultural, economic, and even strategic strings attached to make light of this relationship. Even though the vast majority of Azerbaijan's oil will not be transported via the Russian-dominated "Northern Route," there are still an array of commercial treaties and agreements. The level of trade between both nations has increased considerably, and Russia still believes it can obtain the lion's share of petroleum shipments by reducing pipeline transit fees between Baku and Novorossiysk.

This seems highly unlikely, however, due to an alliance known as GUAAM. Founded in 1996, it is named after its member states: Georgia,

Both halves of Azerbaijan were briefly united during World War II by the Soviet Union, in an attempt to create an "Autonomous Government of Azerbaijan." The United Nations Security Council declared the Soviet action illegal, which resulted in Azerbaijan's continued separation.

Ukraine, Uzbekistan, Azerbaijan, and Moldova. All are former Soviet republics, which banded together in order to strengthen their political and economic sovereignty. Azerbaijan and its cohorts wish to lessen their dependency on Russia's antiquated and largely unreliable transit networks. Establishing a Europe-Caucasus-Asia corridor that bypasses Russian territory is therefore one of GUAAM's major goals. This would not only improve communication with other international markets, but diminish Russia's excessive sway over their business affairs. The Baku-Supsa, or "Western" oil route, is a precursor of what GUAAM intends to accomplish.

While GUAAM has a special partnership with NATO, Russia continues to wield significant power in regional security. The Russian military still operates a major facility in Azerbaijan. Concerned about the growing uncertainties in the nearby Middle East, Azerbaijan recently allowed the base to stay under Russia's control for another ten years. In return, Moscow agreed to stop supporting separatist movements and other activities that threaten the Azerbaijani government.

The relationship with Iran is much tenser. The Iranian government accuses Azerbaijan of illegally surveying for oil in its section of the Caspian Sea. To underscore Iran's annoyance, an Iranian warship fired warning shots toward an Azerbaijani research vessel in July 2001, causing a diplomatic incident between Baku and Tehran. Given the legal uncertainties as to what rights bordering states have in development of the Caspian's resources, Azerbaijan and Iran continue to eye each other warily. A similar

Iranian president Mohammad Khatami (right) meets with Azerbaijani foreign minister Elmar Maharram Mammadyarov in Tehran. Although the relationship between the two countries has been tense since Azerbaijan gained its independence in 1991, recently the countries have tried to improve their diplomatic relations, with Khatami visiting Baku in August 2004.

problem—minus the gunboat diplomacy—exists with Turkmenistan, which has adopted Iran's viewpoint that all oil exploration should be suspended until a general agreement has been reached on the Caspian Sea.

Iran and Azerbaijan also do not see eye to eye on the role Islam should play in their political governance. Although the people of both nations are predominantly Shiite Muslims, Iran allows theological doctrine to greatly influence its policies. Azerbaijan, on the other hand, separates religious philosophy from state affairs.

Another issue affecting both societies is the estimated 13 to 16 million ethnic, or "South," Azerbaijanis living in Iran. Their legacy goes back to the 1828 Treaty of Turkmanchai, which established the border between the

Persian and Czarist Russian Empires. The separation split Azerbaijan's population, creating a national sentiment that longs for eventual reunification. Southern Azerbaijanis have integrated into Iranian society, and even hold some senior political positions, but any calls for a greater autonomy are quickly suppressed. Azeri-language publications have been banned in Iran, and there are worries about a concerted effort by Iran's government to "Persianize" Azerbaijan's ethnicity.

Reunification, however, is not a primary concern. What does rile Baku is Iran's close political and economic ties with Armenia. This seems like a hypocritical stance to many Azerbaijanis, who feel that while the Iranians avidly support Islamic solidarity, they refuse to condemn Christian Armenia battling fellow Muslims. Although the Iranian government has declared support for Azerbaijan's territorial integrity in the Nagorno-Karabakh conflict, this is generally considered an empty gesture.

Despite such grudges and differences of opinion, Azerbaijan's government understands that the country needs to find a way to get along with Iran. As is the case with Russia, Iran is too important to be completely disregarded. Noting that both nations were essentially left out of the anticipated oil pipeline bonanza, Baku recently agreed to help construct a railway that would connect Russia with Iran. Overall, Azerbaijan does make an effort to get along with its neighbors.

The third regional power is Turkey. Not only do they share similar ethnic identities, but Turkey's secular Muslim philosophy greatly appeals to the Azerbaijanis. It serves as a guideline for the nation's post-Soviet transformation and beyond. Yet there are limits to how much Turkey can influence Azerbaijan. The Turks lack the historical legacies that were left behind by Russia and Iran. The Ottoman Empire never controlled Azerbaijan for more than brief periods of time throughout its 500-year reign. Its successor, the Republic of Turkey, was completely cut off from Azerbaijan and other Turkic republics for nearly 70 years by Soviet rule.

Furthermore, the only part of Azerbaijan that touches Turkey is the enclave of Nakhichevan. Contrast this with the size of Russia and Iran's Azerbaijani borders. Even the two other Transcaucasus nations, Georgia and Armenia, have larger frontiers with Turkey.

In spite of all this, Turkish businessmen are a constant presence in Baku, either searching for new commercial ventures or managing those they already have. Turkey's government is heavily involved in economic development, educational, and even military programs with Azerbaijan. Although throughout the course of Azerbaijan's history Turkey's input has been peripheral, perhaps it will become an intrinsic part of the future.

Atlanticism

Due to the war on terrorism, Azerbaijani relations with the United States have expanded. Prior to September 11, 2001, Washington mainly perceived Azerbaijan's potential oil wealth as a promising alternative to overdependence on energy supplies from the Persian Gulf. The United States diplomatically supported the construction of the Baku-Tbilisi-Ceyhan, or "Southern" pipeline route, for enabling Caspian crude to reach Western markets.

The political connections were less encouraging. The United States has a sizeable population of Armenian descent, who are wary of Azerbaijan. This wariness is a result of the periodic strife that has afflicted both societies throughout history. When riots erupted after the Soviet Union's disintegration, the Armenian community in the United States felt that they had a duty to support their brethren. Some donated money to support the newly independent nation of Armenia, while others notified their Congressional representatives about the unfolding circumstances.

There was not a similar effort from the Azerbaijani side. Those who live in the United States are a smaller and less coordinated group, compared to their Armenian counterparts. Moreover, the vast majority of Azerbaijani

U.S. Secretary of Defense Donald Rumsfeld responds to a question during a joint press briefing in Baku with Azerbaijan's minister of defense, General Safar Abiyev, December 2001. After the September 11, 2001, terrorist attacks on the World Trade Center and Pentagon, the United States established closer ties to Azerbaijan and other secular Muslim states of Central Asia, attempting to enlist them in the fight against Islamist terrorism. Azerbaijan proved its commitment to the war on terrorism by sending troops to Afghanistan and Iraq.

Americans come from Iran, which gives them a different historical background, and they were not emotionally invested in this conflict.

These circumstances did not bode well for Azerbaijan, which became cast as the culprit responsible for igniting communal violence within Nagorno-Karabakh. The U.S. government responded to this alleged misbehavior by placing **sanctions** on Azerbaijan. All public-aid support programs were consequently suspended. This action was generally referred to as Section 907 (based on the document's name), and greatly strained U.S.-Azerbaijani relations. Such vital programs as refugee relief and economic development particularly suffered.

September 11, 2001, altered Washington's outlook toward Azerbaijan. The country's pariah status changed because it was a secular Muslim society willing to fight terrorism. Its location next door to troublesome Iran, a member of what President George W. Bush called the "axis of evil," bolstered this new perception. The United States needed a regional ally that could monitor Iranian movements in the increasingly important, oil-rich Caspian region. Baku willingly obliged, and Washington reciprocated by discontinuing Section 907.

"Eurocentrism"

The third part of Azerbaijan's foreign policy is finding ways that will eventually lead to its becoming a part of Europe. There are encouraging signs from the European Union (EU), the continent's body for setting political, economic, and social policies, that it is interested in closer ties with Azerbaijan. One issue, which both sides agree needs a resolution, is the Nagorno-Karabakh conflict.

May 2004 marked the tenth anniversary of a Russian-brokered cease-fire agreement that ended the fighting. The fact that the truce has held without any international peacekeeping measures surprises analysts and mediators alike. The scars remain, however, and hostilities can resume at any minute. Azerbaijan insists on returning Nagorno-Karabakh under its rule, and Armenia refuses to consider that scenario, or giving back any additional territory it has seized.

The Vienna-based Organization for Security and Cooperation in Europe (OSCE) has been leading negotiations to achieve a mutually agreeable compromise. They have set up an organization known as the Minsk Group, which consists of Russia, the United States, and France, for handling mediation. Despite continuous attempts, it has failed to achieve any worthwhile results.

The Minsk Group came very close to cutting a deal in the spring of 2001. In the Florida community of Key West, talks were held for the purpose of having Azerbaijan recognize Nagorno-Karabakh as part of Armenia. In return for this concession, Armenia would withdraw from all but one of the districts it was occupying within Azerbaijan, and allow the opening of a transport corridor through its territory, which would allow Baku direct access to its Nakhichevan enclave.

Ilham Aliyev addresses the Parliamentary Assembly of the Council of Europe in Strasbourg, France, April 2004. Since gaining independence, a major goal of Azerbaijan's foreign policy has been to become part of Europe.

This accord was never signed, and both sides accused one another of backtracking on promises. The truth of the matter is, however, that whoever signs off on any solution would be branded a traitor by their domestic opponents. Armenian and Azerbaijani authorities both recognize that risking a settlement on Nagorno-Karabakh could lead to destabilizing situations within their countries.

The European Union believes that a new outlook is needed to overcome this stalemate. In order to restart negotiations, they are offering Armenia and Azerbaijan the prospect of greater integration into various EU programs. While Azerbaijanis feel that this might be a European ploy for securing lower Caspian oil prices, Ilham Aliyev has indicated that he would like the EU to be more active in Nagorno-Karabakh mediation efforts.

Europe would be happy to oblige, save for one situation it wishes Azerbaijan to amend. The EU believes that Baku can do better at improving political freedom. Azerbaijan has a contentious relationship with Europe on this matter, especially following the nation's October presidential election, when several members of opposition parties were arrested for protesting the results. The Parliamentary Assembly of the Council of Europe (PACE), an organization that is separate from the EU, has particularly questioned Baku's actions. Azerbaijan has been a member of PACE since 2001, and therefore has to pay special attention to the association's concerns.

While President Aliyev claims that the detainees were committing crimes against the state with violent demonstrations, he has released some that PACE had asserted were political prisoners.

Another European-Azerbaijani connection is the collective security system known as the North Atlantic Treaty Organization (NATO). The Azerbaijanis belong to a particular program within NATO, called the Partnership for Peace (PFP), which offers limited membership to those newly independent states that had once been part of the Soviet Union. PFP members are allowed to participate in NATO military exercises and peacekeeping operations. Azerbaijan has been part of the PFP since 1996, contributing personnel to such NATO endeavors as pacifying the troubled former Yugoslavian province of Kosovo. In return for Azerbaijan's assistance, NATO provides training in air defense, civil-emergency readiness, and other defense-related matters. One area in which NATO has been particularly grateful to Azerbaijan is sharing its information on terrorism. The Azerbaijani government has recently asked for closer cooperation with NATO, hoping its continued assistance will eventually lead to full membership within the prestigious organization.

Ca. 800 B.C.:	The Scythians and Medes move into Southern Azerbaijan.
Ca. 500 B.C.:	Cyrus the Great takes over western Azerbaijan.
330 B.C.:	Alexander the Great defeats Persian forces and absorbs Azerbaijan into his empire.
A.D. 100–300:	The nation of Albania emerges.
Ca. 650:	The Arabs bring Islam to the Transcaucasus.
Ca. 1000–1200:	The Turkic Seljuk dynasty gradually replaces Arab control and establishes Azerbaijan's cultural identity.
Ca. 1200–1400:	The Mongol invasions sweep into Azerbaijan.
Ca. 1400–1500:	Various Khanates govern in the Mongols aftermath.
1501:	The Persian Safavid dynasty is established, under which Shia Islam is introduced and becomes Azerbaijan's state religion.
1700s:	Czarist Russia begins to challenge Persia's rule in the Transcaucasus.
1813:	The Treaty of Gulistan, in which Persia cedes territory north of the Aras River to Russia, is signed.
1828:	Under the Treaty of Turkmanchai, Persia gives up further possessions in Azerbaijan to Czarist Russia, and formally splits the nation into a Russian-controlled northern part, and a Persian-controlled south.
1872:	Russia allows public investment in Azerbaijan's petroleum industry, creating an oil boom.
1905–1907:	The Tatar-Armenian War occurs, reflecting ethnic tensions between Azerbaijanis and Armenians.
1917:	Russia's Czarist monarchy is overthrown.
1918–1920:	After the "March Days" terror ends, the Azerbaijan Democratic Republic is established, beginning the

nation's first independence period. It ends with the overthrow of the republic and start of Soviet rule.

1930s: During the period known as the "Great Terror," thousands of people perish in Joseph Stalin's purges.

1941–1945: During World War II, Baku's oil fields are a major target for Nazi invaders.

1969: Haidar Aliyev becomes the head of the Communist Party of Azerbaijan.

1980s: During the era of *glasnost* and *perestroika*, major reforms are carried out in the U.S.S.R.; Communal violence begins to break out between Armenians and Azerbaijanis over Nagorno-Karabakh.

1989: The Popular Front is formed, advocating major changes in Azerbaijan's relations within the U.S.S.R.

1990: The Soviet government sends troops to Azerbaijan in response to the Nagorno-Karabakh crisis and growing challenges to its authority.

1991: The U.S.S.R. ceases to exist. The independent Republic of Azerbaijan is established.

1992: The Popular Front of Azerbaijan is elected to govern.

1993: Public discontent over the Popular Front's handling of the Nagorno-Karabakh situation brings Haidar Aliyev back to power.

1994: Ceasefire agreement with Armenia ends the fighting over Nagorno-Karabakh. The "contract of the century" is signed with foreign oil companies.

2003: Haidar Aliyev dies. His son Ilham succeeds him amid much political controversy.

2004: Azerbaijan asks the Council of Europe to expel Armenia from the organization.

borderland—land that is located next to another nation's territory.

caliph—the ruler of the Muslim world.

caravanserai—an inn for traveling merchants, who once traveled across Asia, the Middle East, and the Transcaucasus regions.

commissars—those who headed government branches or ministries in the former Soviet Union.

consortium—a business alliance of several companies.

entrepreneur—a person who organizes a commercial undertaking on their own.

indigenous—native to a particular state or country.

isthmus—a narrow strip of land having water at each side and connecting two larger bodies of land.

littoral—land along a shoreline.

mullahs—Islamic religious clerics.

principalities—territories that were ruled by princes.

reserves—something that is kept or stored for later use.

sanctions—boycotts or penalties against a particular nation.

sectarian—devoted to a certain belief or philosophy.

secular—non-religious; relating to a government that is not influenced by religious beliefs.

Sovietization—the forcing of what was the Soviet culture upon others.

Turkic—a subfamily of people and languages which originated in Central Asia and spread to Turkey and Azerbaijan.

vassal—a person who was under the authority of a feudal lord or ruler.

Further Reading

Alstadt, Audrey. *The Azerbaijani Turks: Power and Identity Under Russian Rule*. Stanford, California: Hoover Institution Press, 1992.

Croissant, Cynthia. *Azerbaijan, Oil and Politics*. Commack, New York: Nova Science Publishers, 1998.

De Waal, Thomas. *Black Garden: Armenia and Azerbaijan Through Peace and War*. New York: New York University Press, 2003.

Goltz, Thomas. *Azerbaijan Diary: A Rogue Reporter's Adventures in an Oil-Rich, War-Torn, Post-Soviet Republic*. Armonk, New York: M.E. Sharpe, 1998.

Hemming, Jonathan. *The Implications of the Revival of the Oil Industry in Azerbaijan*. Durham, United Kingdom: University of Durham, 1998.

Heyat, Ferideh. *Azeri Women in Transition: Women in Soviet and Post-Soviet Azerbaijan*. London: Routledge Curzon, 2002.

Landau, Jacob M., and Kellner-Heineke, Barbara. *Politics of Language in Ex-Soviet States: Azerbaijan, Uzbekistan, Kazakhstan, Turkmenistan and Tajikistan*. Ann Arbor: University of Michigan Press, 2001.

Leeuw, Charles van der. *Azerbaijan: A Quest for Identity*. New York: St. Martin's Press, 1989.

Swietochowski, Tadeusz, and Brian C. Collins. *Historical Dictionary of Azerbaijan*. Lanham, Maryland: The Scarecrow Press, 1999.

Swietochowski, Tadeusz. *Russia and Azerbaijan: A Borderland in Transition*. New York, Columbia University Press, 1995.

http://ilham-aliyev.org/index-1024html

Office of Azerbaijan's President (has an English link).

http://azembassy.com/index.html

Informative website of the Embassy of Azerbaijan to the United States.

http://www.azer.com/index.html

Website for Azerbaijan International Magazine.

http://www.bakusun.az:8101/index.html

Baku's English language weekly newspaper for the city's growing foreign community—particularly good for cultural and regional coverage.

http://bakutoday.net/index.php

Excellent online daily newspaper covering Azerbaijan and the Transcaucasus, a project of the AzerNet News Network (ANN).

http://azerb.com/

The most comprehensive source of information on Azerbaijan.

http://azerbaijan.aznet.org/azerbaijan/

Award-winning website dealing with the cultural traditions of Azerbaijan.

http://www.baku-vision.com/

An excellent site about Baku, with lots of great pictures and links.

Index

Numbers in **bold italic** refer to captions.

Index

Picture Credits

The **FOREIGN POLICY RESEARCH INSTITUTE (FPRI)** served as editorial consultants for the GROWTH AND INFLUENCE OF ISLAM IN THE NATIONS OF ASIA AND CENTRAL ASIA series. FPRI is one of the nation's oldest "think tanks." The Institute's Middle East Program focuses on Gulf security, monitors the Arab-Israeli peace process, and sponsors an annual conference for teachers on the Middle East, plus periodic briefings on key developments in the region.

Among the FPRI's trustees is a former Secretary of State and a former Secretary of the Navy (and among the FPRI's former trustees and interns, two current Undersecretaries of Defense), not to mention two university presidents emeritus, a foundation president, and several active or retired corporate CEOs.

The scholars of FPRI include a former aide to three U.S. Secretaries of State, a Pulitzer Prize–winning historian, a former president of Swarthmore College and a Bancroft Prize–winning historian, and two former staff members of the National Security Council. And the FPRI counts among its extended network of scholars—especially its Inter-University Study Groups—representatives of diverse disciplines, including political science, history, economics, law, management, religion, sociology, and psychology.

DR. HARVEY SICHERMAN is president and director of the Foreign Policy Research Institute in Philadelphia, Pennsylvania. He has extensive experience in writing, research, and analysis of U.S. foreign and national security policy, both in government and out. He served as Special Assistant to Secretary of State Alexander M. Haig Jr. and as a member of the Policy Planning Staff of Secretary of State James A. Baker III. Dr. Sicherman was also a consultant to Secretary of the Navy John F. Lehman Jr. (1982–1987) and Secretary of State George Shultz (1988).

A graduate of the University of Scranton (B.S., History, 1966), Dr. Sicherman earned his Ph.D. at the University of Pennsylvania (Political Science, 1971), where he received a Salvatori Fellowship. He is author or editor of numerous books and articles, including *America the Vulnerable: Our Military Problems and How to Fix Them* (FPRI, 2002) and *Palestinian Autonomy, Self-Government and Peace* (Westview Press, 1993). He edits *Peacefacts*, an FPRI bulletin that monitors the Arab-Israeli peace process.

GERALD ROBBINS is an Associate Scholar with the Foreign Policy Research Institute in Philadelphia, Pennsylvania, where he specializes in Turkish affairs. He worked in Azerbaijan, directing political and economic development programs for the non-governmental organization Freedom House. He has written widely for various publications about Turkey and the Transcaucasus region.